ICT in Business

ICT in Business

business and communication systems GCSE for CCEA/ICAA

steve cushing
colin harber stuart
dave parry
pete hutchings

JOHN MURRAY

Acknowledgements

The authors and publishers would like to thank the following sources for permission to reproduce photographs.

Cover Tek Image/Science Photo Library; **p.32** Ron Chapple/ Getty-Images; **p.33** John Townson/Creation; **p.34** Powerstock; **p.38** Dennis Hallinan/Getty-Images; **p.39** Powerstock; **p.42** Ace Photos; **p.54** *(both)* John Townson/Creation; **p.58** Ace Photos; **p.71** Ace Photos; **p.72** Stewart Cohen/Getty-Images; **p.77** Trip Photo Library; **p.80** Trip Photo Library; **p.85** *(all)* Creation; **p.93** Powerstock; **p.94** *(both)* Getty-Images; **p.95** Ace Photos; **p.97** Trip Photo Library; **p.106** Collections; **p.107** Robert Harding Photo Library; **p.121** Ace Photos; **p.122** Trip Photo Library; **p.131** John Townson/Creation; **p.133** John Townson/Creation; **p.134** John Townson/ Creation; **p.136** Ace Photo Library; **p.147** Getty-Images; **p.151** John Townson/Creation; **p.152** John Townson/Creation; **p.153** John Townson/Creation; **p.154** *(both)* John Townson/Creation.

First published in 2002
by John Murray (Publishers) Ltd
50 Albemarle Street
London W1S 4BD

Illustrations by Richard Duszczak, Linden Artists, Wearset Ltd
Layouts by Wearset Ltd
Cover design by John Townson/Creation
Typeset in 12/14pt Galliard by Wearset Ltd, Boldon, Tyne and Wear
Printed and bound by G. Canale, Torino, Italy

A catalogue entry for this title is available from the British Library

ISBN 0 7195 7264 9
Teacher's Notes 0 7195 7265 7

Contents

Section 5: Marketing

Section 6: Finance

Introduction

Computers, and technology based on computers, are an increasingly important part of all of our lives. They are also having a major impact on the ways that businesses carry out their main activities. Initially computers were developed as a 'stand-alone' technology designed to perform specific functions such as sequences of calculations. Today's computers form just one component of Business Communication Systems capable of performing tasks that combine the important human function of communication with the ability to process mountains of business data.

This textbook will help you understand how Business Communication Systems incorporating Information and Communications Technology (ICT) are used in modern business. You will develop your knowledge, understanding and use of modern software applications in a business context. In so doing, you will be introduced to a range of important business ideas.

This book is based on the CCEA/ICAA specification for GCSE Business Communication Systems. However, it is suitable for a wide range of Business, BCS and ICT courses, including vocational or applied GCSEs.

The book starts with a section outlining the main software applications used in most schools and businesses. There are then further sections covering the main functional areas of business. Each section includes a number of tasks designed to develop your understanding of both business theory and ICT applications within business.

We hope that you will enjoy using this book. As a result, you should develop a broad range of the ICT skills required in the business world.

Steve Cushing

Section 1

Use of ICT tools

Publishing software

Word-processors and DTP

Most people who have ever used a computer have probably used publishing software. The two main types of publishing software are **word-processors** and **desktop publishing (DTP)**. Publishing software is also used in most businesses.

Although word-processors and DTP software are becoming increasingly alike, they still have significant differences and it is important that you understand what they are. These differences mean that it is better to carry out some tasks on a word-processor, and others using DTP.

Word-processors were originally designed to enable the user to **enter** and **process** text. They have replaced typewriters as the main way to produce letters and other documents. When you open a word-processor and create a new blank document, you can type text directly onto the page. The text can then be edited to improve its appearance. Word-processors contain many additional functions so that, for example, tables and images can be put onto the page.

DTP was originally designed to enable users to create high quality professional-looking newsletters and leaflets. Most small businesses use DTP to create their publicity material.

Most DTP packages are frame-based. This means that when you enter text it goes into a **text-frame**. When you enter a picture it goes into a **picture-frame**. These frames can be moved around the page so that the **layout** can be improved. Changing the position or size of one frame will not necessarily affect the location of the other frames.

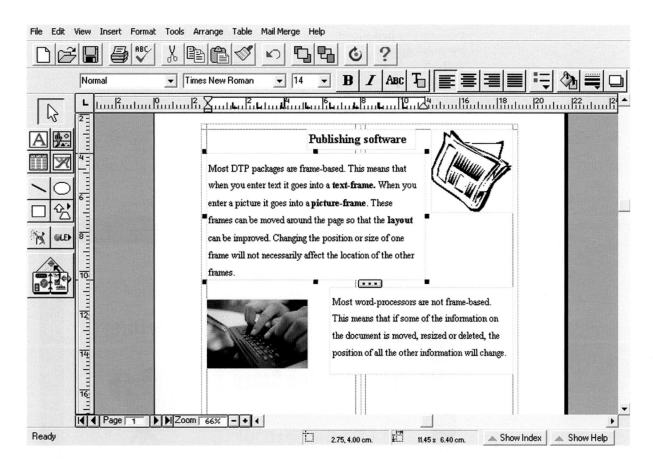

DTP software can be used to arrange pictures and text on the page

Most word-processors are not frame-based. This means that if some of the information on the document is moved, resized or deleted, the position of all the other information will change. This makes them unsuitable for documents requiring lots of graphics.

For this reason it is a good idea to use a word-processor for documents that are mainly text-based and a DTP package for documents that combine text with a lot of other types of data.

The following table (overleaf) gives you an idea of the business documents that can be created using publishing software.

Documents produced by publishing software	Business examples
Letters	Letters to individual customers or mail-shots to all the firm's customers
Notices	Health and safety notices
Leaflets and posters	Publicity leaflets informing customers of new products
Reports	Financial reports such as cash flow, and profit and loss
Booklets	Training manuals and staff handbooks

Publishing software can help a business make a good impression

Grand Opening!

You are invited to the **opening** of

Holly's Video Store

23 Grange Street
Midgeley

Store opens March 14^(th).

We have hundreds of videos, DVDs and computer games for you to rent.

Special opening offer: rent two videos for the price of one!

Holly's, you wouldn't want to miss it!

Benefits and drawbacks of publishing software

There are a number of benefits to businesses of using publishing software.

- High quality, professional-looking documents can be produced.
- Documents can be saved on the computer's backing store. This means rows of large filing cabinets no longer need take up valuable office space.
- Saved documents can be retrieved and edited to create new documents. This is much quicker than creating a new document from scratch.
- Templates of commonly used documents can be created – for example, a document containing the business's letterhead and space to write the letter. The **template** can then be used to create new letters quickly.

These benefits mean that work can be carried out more quickly, with fewer staff, and using less space than before. This can help to reduce the firm's costs and make the business more efficient.

Unfortunately, there are still some disadvantages to using publishing software in business. For example, the initial cost of buying and installing computers and software can be high and staff need to be trained to use them. The computers then cost money to maintain, repair and upgrade to new and better versions.

Each business needs to weigh up the costs and benefits of using computers. They will do this by estimating how much the computer system will cost the business and comparing this with the estimated improvement in profits that will result. If the computer system is cost-effective the firm will invest in the technology.

Features of publishing software packages

There are many different publishing software packages available. They all have the same basic features, but work in slightly different ways. This book cannot tell you how to use the software available to you, but will try to explain how the type of software is used and the benefits of using the technology. All the tasks described below can be performed by most word-processors and desktop publishing packages.

Enter text

Text can be arranged and styled to help make the meaning clear to the reader

Text can be typed into a blank or pre-formatted document, and then adjusted to suit the needs of the user. For example, the font, size or style of the text can be altered. Individual blocks of text can be edited by selecting them. This is done by using the **mouse** to highlight the text.

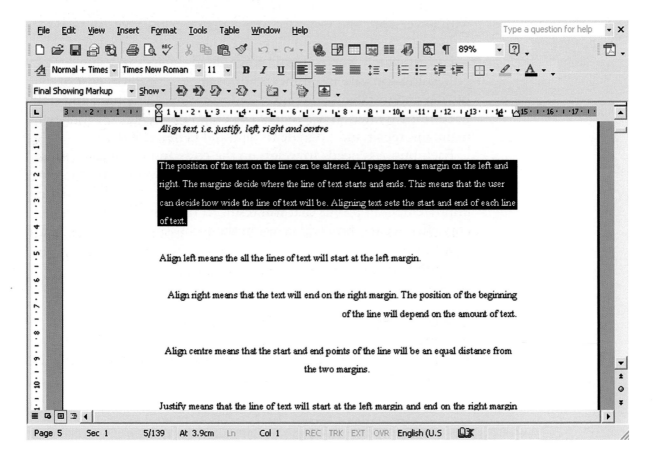

Copy and paste text

It's possible to copy a block of text, usually by first highlighting it using the cursor. This text can then be pasted – in other words, added – to another part of the same document. This method can also be used to copy data to different files.

Cut and paste text

Text can be moved to a new location in the document, or even to a different document, in the same way as copying. The text is first highlighted, then cut out of the document and placed on the computer's **clipboard** (a place where it can temporarily store a piece of data). The data is then pasted from the clipboard into its new location.

Align text – justify, left, right and centre

The position of the text on the line can be altered. All pages have a margin on the left and the right. The margins decide where the line of text starts and ends. This means that the user can decide how wide the line of text will be. Aligning text sets the start and end of each line of text.

> 'Align left' means that all the lines of text will start at the left margin.
>
> 'Align right' means that the text will end at the right margin. The position of the beginning of the line will depend on the amount of text.
>
> 'Align centre' means that the start and end points of the line will be an equal distance from the two margins.
>
> 'Justify' means the line of text will start at the left margin and end at the right margin, and the spaces between words will be adjusted so that the words fit the line exactly.

The conventional view is that left justified text looks best for informal documents such as letters and notices and justified text is best for formal documents like reports. Newspapers and magazines usually use justified text alignment.

Incorporate clip-art/graphic images

Images can help to improve the appearance of the document. There are two main types of image:

- **clip-art**, which is usually installed with the publishing software
- images created by the user through painting software or scanning and digital photography.

Images usually need to be created or stored in a different piece of software and then imported into the publishing package.

The main thing to remember about images is that they need to be appropriate to the document. An image should only be used if it can communicate the message better than text.

Prepare and insert a table

Tables are a useful way of presenting data that has some structure – for example, a list of products and their prices. Most publishing software enables you to add and remove rows or columns. You can also format the appearance of the table.

Use text-wrapping around images

Pictures are rarely so big that they need to occupy the entire width taken up by a row of text on a page. Text-wrapping enables the text to 'flow' around the picture, so the space left by the picture is filled with text. This makes the document look much more professional.

Use text boxes and text flow

Text boxes are a good way to display a piece of text that is relevant to the main text on the page, but makes a separate point. Text-wrapping can be used so that the main text flows around the text box.

Use headers and footers

There are a number of ways that documents can be made to work more efficiently, as well as look more professional.

Headers and footers are lines of information that appear at the top (header) or bottom (footer) of a page. The information is usually something about the document – for example, who wrote it and when it was printed. Information put onto the header or footer will appear on every page of the document. Most publishing software will also add the page number and update it automatically as the user adds new pages.

Use bullet points and paragraph numbering

A list can be made to stand out if a symbol or bullet point identifies each separate point. Sometimes the list needs to be numbered – most publishing software can insert the numbers automatically. Formal business reports often give different numbers to each paragraph. For example, paragraph 3.5.7 would be the seventh paragraph in the fifth section of the third chapter. Again, these numbers can be entered automatically.

Use mail-merge facilities

Mail-merge is a quick way of producing separate letters for a number of people, all containing the same text, but each showing the individual recipient's name and address.

For example, a company could send a letter to all its customers informing them of a new product. Each customer's name can be inserted into the letter to make it seem more personal. The user creates a standard letter containing the text to go into all the letters, and a separate database to store the customers' personal details (names, addresses and so on). Codes are placed into the letter where the each customer's data will be inserted, using the symbols < and >. For example, the letter could begin 'Dear <first name>'. The standard letter can then be merged with the database so that each letter is personalised.

Other features

Other useful features of publishing software you need to know about include:

■ spell check, grammar check and thesaurus – these help you to improve the quality of your writing
■ word count – this counts the number of words in a document
■ drawing tools – these allow you to create your own simple drawings directly into the document.

How to use publishing software to produce beautiful-looking pages

Publishing software allows you to create attractive-looking pages for your school work. So why not use it?

You should practise using the basic functions of your word-processor to improve the presentation of your ICT work. Below is a list of suggested guidelines for how you should present your work.

Remember, it's not just what you say that counts, but how you say it!

A. Fonts

The main font used on most publishing software is Times New Roman - it's what this guide is written in. Some people like this font. They think it makes the text easier to read. Avoid sans-serif fonts such as Arial or Helvetica: these can make continuous reading more difficult.

You should use different font styles to improve the layout - the use of **bold**, *italics* and underlining all help. But you should avoid doing them ***all at once***.

In most cases, the *size* of font chosen should be eleven or twelve points. This will be easy to read, when printed out on A4 paper.

B. New Sentences

Some people like to leave just one space between a full stop and the first letter of the next sentence. Other people like to insist on two spaces. Whichever method you choose you must be consistent.

C. Paragraphs

New paragraphs should begin like this one, with a double-line space between it and the last paragraph.

You should not begin a new paragraph like this.

D. Justification

You have two choices. Justification arranges your text in a straight line on both the left and right hand margins. Left-aligned will be straight only on the left, leaving the text 'ragged' on the right. This has the advantage of producing more regular word-spacing - but justification will probably have a better visual effect overall. This document uses justification.

E. Indentation

Never adjust your indentation using the spacebar. This will create very uneven layout when you print your document. *Always* use the TAB stop (top left of keyboard) and the INDENT function (found on the formatting toolbar in Word). Remember that a TAB stop indents just the first line of a paragraph. The INDENT function will indent the whole of the paragraph.

F. Headers and footers

Use these to insert page numbers and things like the filename and date. You can use them to put your name on the page as well. Headers and footers will appear at the top and bottom of the page when you print your document.

G. Widows and orphans

In laying out your pages, you should avoid creating paragraphs which start on the last line of a page or which finish on the first of the next. (These are called 'widows' and 'orphans'.) An extra space at the bottom of a page is more acceptable than just one or two lines of text at the top of the next, so take text over to the next page. One way to do this is to enter a page-break where *you* want the page to end.

H. Page appearance

If you have done all of the above then you'll probably produce good-looking work. But before you print you should make sure that all of the pages look attractive. Put your pages to the test by asking yourself the following questions.

1 Have I checked the spelling by proof-reading the pages, and using the spell checker?
2 Is the page attractive to look at? Is there too much 'white space' (the gaps on the page where there is nothing)?
3 Is the page too cluttered? Would it be better to use an extra page and spread the material out more?
4 Could I improve the appearance by adding pictures or graphics?
5 Are there any widows or orphans?
6 Has it got my name on it?

You can use word-processing or DTP software to dramatically improve your presentation

2 | Spreadsheets

A **spreadsheet** is a program that allows you to store data that has been organised in some structured way. It is also possible to enter commands that enable the spreadsheet to change or manipulate the data. The result is that the user can see the effects of one change on the data collection as a whole. Spreadsheets can also convert numerical data into graphs and charts. This makes them particularly useful for generating graphics to go into business reports.

A spreadsheet is organised into rows and columns. The rows and columns intersect to form a grid. The grid is made up of individual cells. Each column has a heading letter and each row has a heading number. These are combined to give the reference for each individual cell. The cell references work in the same way as the co-ordinates on a map. For example, cell B4 is in the second column and the fourth row. Cell C4 is one to the right of B4 and C5 is one below C4.

In the cell references, the letter always comes first and the number second

Each cell can contain one of the following:

■ input data – for example, the price of a product
■ a command called a function or formula – this instructs the computer as to how you want to manipulate the data. The results of a command, called output data, are displayed in the cell.

Uses of spreadsheets	Business examples
Performing simple calculations	Converting daily sales data into weekly or monthly totals
	Calculating a worker's weekly wage
	Producing a cash flow forecast
Making simple decisions	Deciding whether the business needs to re-order any raw materials
Producing charts	Displaying the weekly sales totals as a bar graph
	Comparing predicted cash flow with the actual figures

Spreadsheets are extremely useful in business for tasks such as accountancy

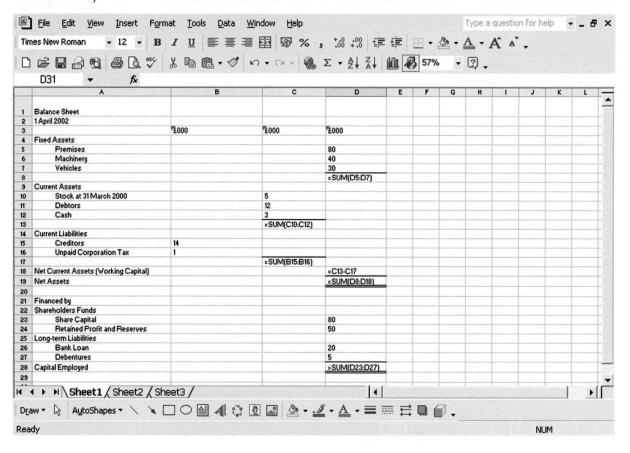

Features of spreadsheet software

Alter cell format

Spreadsheet data can be formatted in a similar way to text formatting in publishing software. For example, the font, size and style of the text in the spreadsheet cells can be altered.

You can also change the format of the spreadsheet itself. This can be done before or after data is entered. The user can change the height of rows or the width of columns. This is useful if some data – for example, someone's last name – is too long to fit into a cell.

The user can specify the type of data to be entered into a cell. For example, a cell that is to show the price of a product can be set to display the numerical data it contains as currency – the user enters 3.99 and the spreadsheet automatically displays this as £3.99. Most spreadsheets will also convert numbers into dates, if required. For example, enter 30-9 and the spreadsheet will display it as September 30th.

Copy and paste data, move or delete data

As with publishing software, data that needs to be entered more than once can be copied from one cell and pasted into another. Data can also be deleted and new data inserted between existing cells. Whole columns or rows can be added or deleted as well. This might have the effect of shifting the remaining data into new cells.

Fill down/across

A quick way to enter similar data into adjoining cells is to use the 'fill down' or 'fill across' command. This can be used to enter the same formula into a number of cells very quickly. In this way, very large spreadsheets can be created in very little time. A similar effect is achieved by using the 'fill handle' on the bottom of the cell that contains the data you want to copy.

Some spreadsheets will recognise a pattern in the information you want to create and change the copied data automatically. For example, you might want to enter the label 'Product 1' in cell A1, 'Product 2' in cell A2 and so on. The spreadsheet will recognise the pattern and put 'Product 3' into cell A3 automatically.

Use formulas and functions

Formulas and functions are the main processes that the spreadsheet will carry out on the input data. To create formulas in a spreadsheet, follow these steps.

1 Select the cell that will contain the result of the calculation (the output cell).
2 Tell the spreadsheet you are building a formula by entering an 'equals' sign (=).
3 Write the formula.

The main symbols used are:

$\times$ multiply by
/ divide by
+ add
– subtract
() perform the instruction inside the brackets first

The most common functions are the following:

SUM(XX:YY)	adds together all the numbers in the cells XX to YY
AVERAGE(XX:YY)	calculates the average (arithmetic mean) of all the numbers in the cells XX to YY
MIN(XX:YY)	displays the smallest number in a series of numbers
MAX(XX:YY)	displays the largest number in a series of numbers
IF(XX<50,"Yes","No")	displays the word 'Yes' if the data in cell XX is less than 50 or 'No' if it isn't. (XX = column heading letter followed by row heading number)

This example shows a simple spreadsheet. Sheet 1 shows the input and output data. Sheet 2 shows the formulas used to calculate the results.

	A	B	C
1	1.3	4	5.2
2	2.4	3	7.2
3	3.2	3	9.6
4	7.3	4	29.2
5	14.2		51.2

Sheet 1

	A	B	C
1	1.3	4	=SUM(A1*B1)
2	2.4	3	=SUM(A2*B2)
3	3.2	3	=SUM(A3*B3)
4	7.3	4	=SUM(A4*B4)
5	=SUM(A1:A4)		=SUM(C1:C4)

Sheet 2

Uses of spreadsheets

A spreadsheet is often used to carry out the following operations.

Creating charts

Data on monthly sales revenue could be shown as a bar chart or line graph

All spreadsheet programs contain a chart function. This can be used to display the contents of the spreadsheet as a number of different types of chart. It is important to create the appropriate chart for the data, as shown in the example.

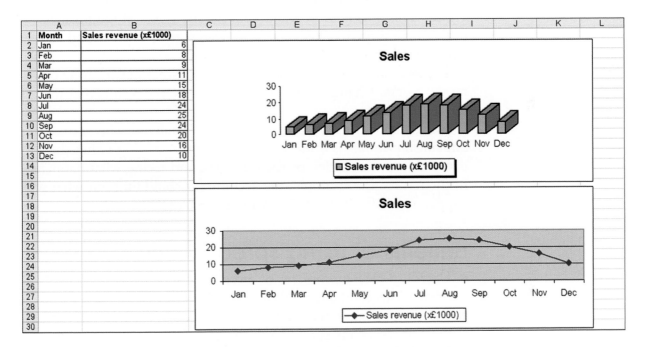

Most spreadsheets allow you to build up the chart step by step. For example, there are options to include a key (legend), a title, and labels for the axes. It is important to include these, otherwise the person who reads the chart may be confused over which data it contains.

Modelling and 'what-if analysis'

A **model** is a simplified representation of a real-life object or event. In Design and Technology, you may have built a scale model of an object. Models can be tested to see how they behave and what the results of a particular design decision will be. This knowledge can help the designer to build the real thing.

Computer models are similar except that they are based on formulas and functions. For example, an accountant could build a spreadsheet to model the impact of increasing wages on the firm's profits. This information could help the managers of the business decide on a wage increase that would keep both workers and the employers happy.

The functions and formulas are the 'rules' that govern how the model works. Changing the rules will change the results that the model produces.

Models allow users to carry out 'what-if analysis'. This sounds difficult but in fact is quite simple. It means changing either the data fed into the model, or the formulas, and seeing what happens to the results. For example, the accountant could find out what will happen to profits if the wage increase is 5% or 10%.

Benefits of using spreadsheets

- Users can create templates of often-used spreadsheets, so that calculations can be carried out very quickly.
- Data can be manipulated with a high level of accuracy, as long as the correct data is entered and the correct formulas are used.
- Calculations can be carried out automatically, so fewer staff might be needed as a result.
- Spreadsheets allow the firm to build models to find out the effects of taking different business decisions.

■ *ICT Activity*

A video store incorporating a console game hire business used a basic spreadsheet to help work out monthly returns and present them to its accountant.

This involved recording data on numbers of videos hired, charge for hiring, number of videos sold and purchase price, with similar data on the console games.

Each day the data was entered onto a spreadsheet, the totals calculated and the sheet then saved. At the end of the week, usually on Sunday evening when the shop was quiet, the week's totals were calculated and the sheet cleared ready for the next week's data. After four weeks of carrying this out, the monthly totals were recorded and sent to the accountant.

Unfortunately, at the end of one tax year the records were not complete, and as the shop owner had not kept each of the weekly records it was difficult to work out the tax bill for the company.

This lead to a more appropriate system being developed, where the data was recorded as before, but instead of wiping the data each week, the spreadsheet covered the whole year, making it easy to see at a glance the total sales and hiring of videos and games.

The data was backed up nightly so that there was always a copy stored away from the shop.

With further development of this spreadsheet, the shop owner was able to produce charts for different time periods – weekly, fortnightly, monthly and so on – which showed trends in sales and hiring. Over the course of a year, this improved the shop owner's ability to stock the shop with appropriate levels of videos and games.

The shop owner felt that the investment of time and the minimal cost of setting up this system was of great benefit. So did the accountant!

Tasks

Create a simple spreadsheet to enable the store to calculate its monthly income from hiring and selling videos.

1 Your spreadsheet will need the following headings:

- video title
- number of times the video was hired
- charge for hiring the video
- total income from hiring the video
- number of copies of the video sold
- purchase price
- total income from selling the video
- total income from hiring and selling the video

2 Enter formulas to enable the spreadsheet to calculate the three income figures for each video.
3 Enter data for about ten video titles.
4 Copy the income formulas down the spreadsheet.
5 Add a formula to calculate the total monthly income from all the video titles.
6 Use formatting to improve the appearance of the spreadsheet.
7 Describe how this spreadsheet could be extended to include data from hiring console games.
8 Describe how this simple spreadsheet could be extended to include more than one month's figures.
9 The shop owner would like to produce a graph comparing the total income of each video title. What would be the best type of graph to use? Give a reason for your answer.

3 Databases

All businesses need to store large amounts of information – for example, details of customers, employees and financial records.

Storing this data can be a problem. Large amounts of paper need to be stored in large filing cabinets. Documents can be easily misplaced. Finding a specific document can be time consuming, and only one person can use the document at any one time. Any reports or calculations that require information from lots of different documents can take a long time to produce.

Computerised databases solve many of these problems. A **database** is any place where data is stored and organised in a structured way. Computerised databases store the data in the computer's memory. The computer can find and process the data very quickly. As a result, information can be retrieved from the database and reports generated highly efficiently.

Uses of databases	Business examples
Storing large amounts of data	Storing customer records
	Storing product details
	Storing a list of all the components needed to make the firm's products
Searching for data that meets certain criteria	Locating a particular customer
	Finding out how much stock of a particular product the firm has got left
	Finding all customers who haven't purchased anything this year
Producing reports	Producing a marketing report to show the areas in which the firm's sales have increased (or decreased)

Benefits and drawbacks of computer databases

The benefits to businesses of using computer databases include the following.

■ Large volumes of data can be stored in a small space.
■ The database can be searched to obtain specific information very quickly.
■ The information remains stored on the database so there is less chance of it being misplaced than if records were stored in separate paper files.
■ The database can process the data so that reports and calculations can be produced quickly and easily.
■ It can be possible for more than one user to see and process the data at the same time.

There are some problems associated with databases, however.

■ Databases can be expensive to build and install.
■ Large databases need expensive computer systems to operate them.
■ Staff need to be trained in how to use the database.
■ Databases need constant updating, otherwise the information they contain will become out of date and therefore less useful.

Structure of a database

All databases have the same basic structure – they are organised into fields and records. A **record** is a complete list of all the data about an individual data-subject (for example, a customer). The data is divided up into different categories or **fields**. For example, details about a customer can be divided into 'first name', 'last name', 'address', 'telephone number', 'account number'. The business will hold the same categories of information about all of its customers. It is easiest to understand this structure when the database is viewed as a table. The fields are the columns of data and each row of data is a record.

An extract from a database showing a firm's customers

	A	B	C	D	E
1	First Name	Last Name	Address	Telephone	Account number
2	John	Smith	9 Baker Street	01902 234567	456845
3	Mark	Smith	23 High Road	01902 232212	456846
4	John	Brown	54 Lower Street	01902 234859	456847

In order to find an individual record quickly it is important to have one item of data that is unique to each record. This data is stored in the **key field**. For example, in the database of a firm's customers shown on page 20, lots of data-subjects will be called Smith, but only one will have the account number 456845. So, in this database 'account number' would be the key field.

Sometimes the key field is used to connect up different databases. For example, the firm could also have a sales database. This could store data on the products that the firm has sold. One of the fields could then be the customer account number. This would enable the firm to see who has bought each product.

Each set of related fields and records is stored in a **file**. For example, customer records could be stored in the customer file, product details in the product file and employee details in the employee file.

A database that stores the data in a number of connected data files is called a **relational database**. **Flat-file databases** store all the data inside a single file. Flat-file databases are much simpler to design than relational databases. What most people think of as a database is usually a simple flat-file database.

Creating a database

In order to create a database, you need to carry out the following tasks.

1 Decide what data needs to be stored in the database.
2 Organise the data into fields. How specific you want the fields to be will depend on how you want to search for data. For example, you could put the whole address as a complete field. But then it would not be possible to search the database for a particular town.
3 Decide whether to use a flat-file or relational database.
4 Decide how to collect the data. This might involve using a data capture form, which often looks like a questionnaire. Customers are asked to fill it in and the data is then transferred onto the database by hand. A lot of websites collect data from visitors in this way – visitors complete a data collection form on-line, and the data then goes straight onto a database.
5 Create the database. With most databases you need to create the files and fields first. Each field needs a name, a data type and a length. The data type is important (the main ones are shown in the table on page 22). For example, most database programs cannot add together the data contained in two fields containing text.

Data type	What it can store	What processes can be carried out	Example of data
Text	Stores text or numeric information	Search for data beginning with/ containing a specific letter Sort data into alphabetical order	Surname Town
Numerical	Stores numbers only	Searches Calculations Sorting into ascending/ descending order	Telephone number Price Age Shoe size
Date	Stores data as a calendar date	As for numerical data, but based on a calendar year	Date of birth Date last sold
Linked objects	Stores data created in other programs	Search for specific objects	Photographs of products Personnel photographs

The field length is also important. This controls how much data can be entered into a field. For example, some banks have customer databases that only allow a surname of 19 characters, or data entries. 'Benjamin B Brown' needs 16 data entries (including spaces). The national telephone directory for England has approximately 55 million residential and business listings, requiring over 1100 million data entries! Field lengths often have to be limited because all this data must be stored in memory, and memory is expensive.

6 Once the fields have been created the data can then be entered. This is usually done one record at a time. In order to ensure that the data entered is likely to be correct, a data validation check can be carried out. This is an automatic check by the computer to make sure that the data is of the right type. For example, if entering a date of birth the database could check that the date is less than (that is, before) the current date. This will not ensure that the data is accurate, but it will check that it is of the correct type.

7 Once entered, the data can be amended. The three main amendments are to enter new data, delete existing data or update a piece of data.

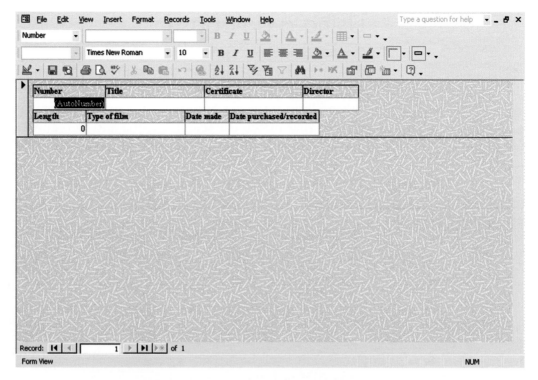

Once the database is set up, to add a new record you input data using a screen like this one

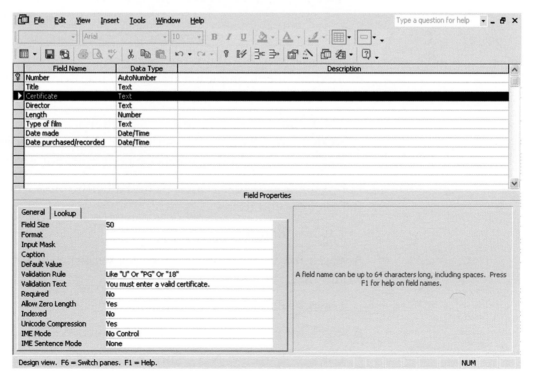

This screen shows the field properties in a database of information about video films

Using a database

'Search and report' is the most common process carried out on a database. The user instructs the database to look for and display specific data.

Searching is the act of looking through the database for the records that match the search criteria and the report is the output from the search. The report could be screen-based or printed.

Search

Search criteria are listed in the table below.

Search criteria	Symbol	Description
Equals	=	Finds records matching a specific value
Less than	<	Finds records whose value is less than the specified amount
Greater than	>	Finds records whose value is greater than the specified amount
Not equal to	<> or =/	Finds records whose value is not equal to the specified amount
Less than or equal to	<=	Finds records whose value is less than or equal to the specified amount
Greater than or equal to	>=	Finds records whose value is greater than or equal to the specified amount

A simple search will use one criterion. A complex search will use more than one. Complex searches also use **Boolean logic** to help the computer decide whether a piece of data meets the criteria:

AND   finds data that meets two criteria
NOR   finds data that doesn't meet either of the criteria
NOT   finds data that meets one criterion but not the other

For example, a simple search to find all customers who live in Barnsley, would use:

Town = 'Barnsley'

A search for all customers in Barnsley with the surname Williams would use:

Town = 'Barnsley' AND Surname = 'Williams'

A search for everyone in Barnsley *not* called Williams would use:

Town = 'Barnsley' NOT Surname = 'Williams'

(The search Town = 'Barnsley' AND Surname =/ 'Williams' would give the same result.)

Report

Reports can also be generated. It is possible to specify which fields the report will show. For example, you might want to display the address and telephone number of each customer in Barnsley called Williams, found as a result of the search above.

Reports can also structure the output data in specific ways. The most common way to structure the output data is to put it into alphabetical or numerical order. For example, the report could list the data alphabetically by surname (Akhtar before Bennett) or numerically by account number.

The input form for a simple database of a telesales company's employees. This form is completed for each new record.

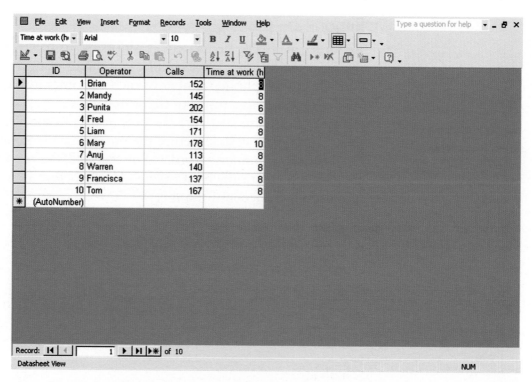

This simple database has ten records, and four fields.

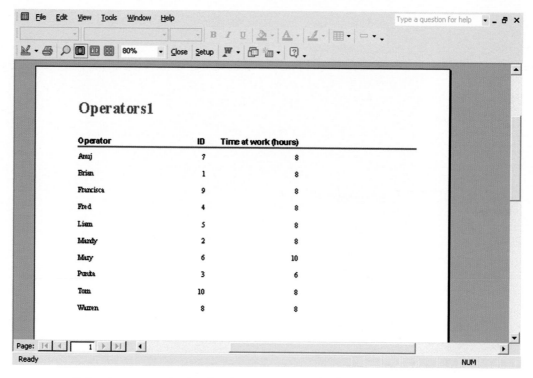

Following a search, the database program displays a report, arranged in alphabetical order.

■ *ICT Activity*

Computers are becoming more widely used at home as well as in business. One of the most common uses is to store addresses and contact details.

The average household sends approximately 100 Christmas cards. They also have to deal with at least three major utility companies, doctors, dentists, vets and various other professionals, not including work colleagues and contacts.

So they need to have available over 150 names, addresses, telephone numbers and other details, as well as important dates such as birthdays and anniversaries.

Although this information can be stored on paper, there are a number of software packages available to record and manipulate such data, enabling retrieval and interrogation.

E-mail software often has a built-in address book, which can be used to store postal addresses and contact details alongside the e-mail address.

Tasks

1 Design a database to store the name, address, e-mail and birthday details of everyone in your class. Remember that memory costs money, so try to design the data fields to record the information in an economic fashion.
2 Enter the data and carry out validation checks.
3 Carry out a search of the database to find the names of the students who live in the same town as the school.

Communications software

The most important business growth area at the beginning of the 21st century is the **internet**. There are two main parts to the internet: the **world wide web**, where web pages provide information and services to users; and electronic mail (**e-mail**).

World wide web

Websites have made it far easier to access information about organisations

Many businesses have their own **website** where customers can find out about the firm's products. Customers can **browse** through the site and **download** information such as product specifications and price structures. Many sites now allow customers to buy products on-line.

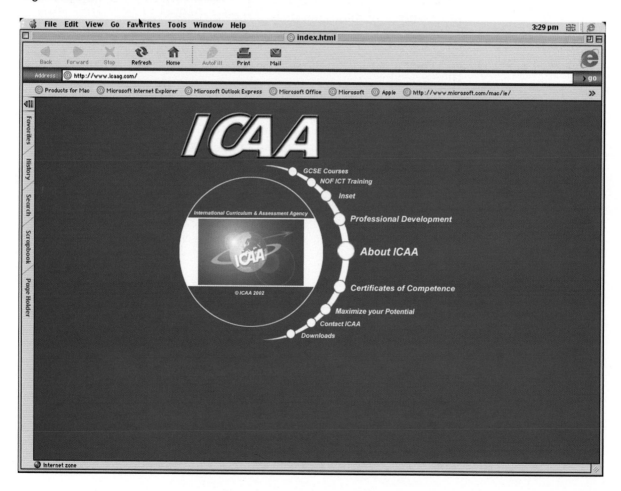

There are also a number of internet-only businesses. These firms do not sell to customers through shops but only via their website. Businesses that combine a traditional range of shops *and* internet retailing are called 'bricks and clicks' firms.

To access a website, a user needs certain **hardware** to connect to the internet, usually a **modem** connected to a telephone line, and a piece of **software** called a **browser**. The browser displays the web pages.

The main features of a website are described in Unit 5.

Searching the web

There are millions of pages of information on the world wide web. So it is important to know how to search for what you want. The main methods are described below.

1 Use the website address

The website address is also known as the uniform resource locator or **URL**. A website address is made up of a number of parts. Take for example the address www.icaag.co.uk:

- 'www' tells the computer that the file can be found by connecting to the world wide web of the internet
- 'icaag' tells the computer to look for the file on the website of an organisation that has registered the name 'icaag' (this may not be the organisation's actual name – it is often an abbreviation of the full name)
- 'co.uk' tells the computer that the website belongs to a business ('co' is short for 'company') in the United Kingdom.

Each part of the address is separated from the others by a full stop.

Names of files contained within the website are written after a forward slash symbol (/). So, for example, www.icaag.co.uk/products would link to a file called 'products' on the icaag website.

2 Search for the website using a search engine

A **search engine** is a website that stores data about other websites. It's best to think of search engines as large databases. Users search for specific websites by using search criteria. It is possible to carry out a simple search, or more complex searches based on **Boolean logic** (Unit 3). For example, you could search for all websites containing information about 'ICT', or you could search for 'ICT AND GCSE'. A customer could search for businesses selling MP3 players by using the keywords 'MP3 player AND retail'.

3 Follow hyperlinks

A **hyperlink** is an instruction to the computer to jump to a new website or web page. The hyperlink contains the URL of the website but it could be displayed as something else – for example, a button labelled 'to visit a great site click here'. (Hyperlinks in text documents are usually blue and underlined.)

4 Use bookmarks or favourites

'Bookmarks' and 'favourites' are different names for the same thing. A browser can store the URL of any website or web page visited. These 'favourite' URLs are stored and organised rather like a telephone directory. To visit a website, you simply select the bookmark or favourite you want from the list.

Benefits and drawbacks of websites

There are many benefits to businesses of having a website.

- Customers can find out about the company and order products from home.
- The business can make contact with potential customers anywhere in the world.
- Visitors to the site can download information from it.
- It can be cheaper to put product details on the website than to send a printed copy of a brochure via the post.
- Information can be updated quickly and economically.
- On-line purchases can be made without sales staff to take the order.

As well as benefits, there are problems associated with having a website.

- The website will cost time and money to create.
- Once created it is important that the website is kept up to date, which can be very time-consuming.
- It costs money to connect a business website to the internet. The website needs to be connected to the internet via a **file-server**. Small businesses find it too expensive to have their own server and instead pay to be connected to an internet service provider (**ISP**).
- A popular website can get thousands of hits (visitors) per day, so the server must have enough capacity for that many people to access it. Increasing capacity costs money, so popular websites can be expensive to run.
- It is possible for people to download and copy information from the website without permission. In the UK, unauthorised use of copied computer material is covered by the Copyright Designs and Patents Act. (Unit 9 covers this in greater detail.)

E-mail

Businesses also use electronic mail (e-mail) to communicate with customers, suppliers and employees.

E-mail is a way of sending and receiving computer data across the telephone network. Simple e-mail messages contain just plain text but it is also possible to attach complete files from any other software.

One way that firms use e-mail is to exchange copies of documents. For example, a marketing manager might prepare a draft version of a report investigating the possibility of launching a new product. This draft report is then e-mailed to a number of people in the marketing department. They read the report, add comments to it and e-mail it back to the manager. The manager then reads the comments and prepares a final version of the report.

Benefits and drawbacks of e-mail

The main benefits of using e-mail are listed below.

- E-mail can be used to send a message instantly to another person anywhere in the world, as long as they have an e-mail address.
- Multiple copies of e-mails can be sent to lots of different people. This is much quicker and cheaper than posting thousands of copies of a **mail-shot**.
- Businesses can use e-mail to communicate directly with their employees.
- E-mail can be used to send copies of computer files – these are added to the basic text message and so are known as **attachments.**
- E-mail can be much cheaper than using the postal service.

There are some problems with e-mail. Attachments can contain computer viruses. A computer **virus** is a program that corrupts or damages other computer files. Attachments should therefore only be downloaded if you trust the source. It is possible to scan a file using **anti-virus software**. However, anti-virus software must be kept up to date as new viruses are developed daily and the software can only detect viruses that it knows about!

Other communications technologies

As well as the internet, there are other communications technologies that a business can use.

Video-conferencing

Also known as teleconferencing, this enables people in different locations to see and talk with each other. The main equipment needed is a video camera and microphone, a display **monitor** and a modem to transmit the data across the telephone network.

Video-conferencing can save a great deal on travel expenses

One benefit of video-conferencing is that people no longer need to travel to meetings. They can stay in their office and still hold meetings with people who are perhaps thousands of miles away. This reduces business costs because travel and accommodation are not needed.

Facsimile transmissions

A facsimile (**fax**) machine converts a printed document into digital data that can be transmitted across the telephone network. At the other end, a fax machine decodes the data back into visual form and prints a copy of the original document. In this way, documents such as letters and drawings can be transmitted to a different location very quickly. Although the technology is different, the effect is the same as sending an e-mail attachment.

Many computers are capable of transmitting a fax, but the majority of faxes are sent from a separate fax machine, which may or may not be combined with a telephone function.

Fax machines are useful when you need to send a hard copy of a document instantly

■ *ICT Case study*

The average day in the office has changed dramatically with the advent of reliable, cost-effective electronic communication.

Sue is a receptionist at a County Council office. Her day starts at 9.00 am.

9.00–9.15	check in post from Royal Mail
9.15–10.00	log on to **intranet**; check and respond to e-mail received overnight, or earlier today
10.00–11.00	check through faxes and carry out photocopying requests
11.00–11.20	tea break (chance to send text message to her husband to arrange who will pick up her daughter from school)
11.20–1.00	typing up minutes from meetings held during the previous days
1.00–1.30	lunch taken at her desk, answering phone calls and noting requests for information
1.30–3.00	updating data files and responding to e-mails, phone calls and written requests for information
3.00	home

Tasks

1 Choose three activities carried out by Sue and describe what ICT she may have been using.
2 Describe how the productivity of Sue's day has been improved through using ICT.
3 Explain the impact that the use of ICT has had upon the Sue's job.

5 | Multimedia

Multimedia means information that is presented in different forms – for example, text, still or moving images, and sound. Multimedia software can be used to create presentations. It can also be used to build websites.

Presentations

A **presentation** is a way of communicating information to an audience. The information can either be informative, where the aim is to let the audience make up their own minds about the information, or persuasive, where the aim is to influence what people think.

Businesses use presentations for many different reasons. For example, a marketing manager might make a presentation to the board of directors about a possible new product. The marketing manager will try to persuade the directors that the new product will be profitable.

The most common type of presentation is where a speaker talks to a group of people. The information is displayed on a screen using a projector and the speaker gives the presentation standing in front of the display. Presentation software can be used to create the display.

A clear and memorable presentation can make a big difference to what people think about a business idea

Presentation software also enables a commentary to be recorded alongside the display. This means that the speaker does not need to be there when the presentation is given. The presentation can, for example, be made available for people to download from the internet and view on their own computers.

Slides

Multimedia presentation software builds up the presentation as a series of linked 'slides', each slide containing information about a particular part of the presentation.

The information can appear on the slide at different times. For example, the speaker might want to take the audience through a number of different points. The points could be displayed all at once as a list of bullet points, or each new point could be added to the list sequentially. Information can appear and then disappear when it is no longer needed.

Text and images can be combined. Each slide, for example, might contain the company logo. Movie clips can be added, as well as hyperlinks to connect to the internet.

It is possible to set the transition time automatically – this is the time for which each slide is displayed before it is replaced by the next part of the presentation. This is useful if the presentation is being given without a speaker. It is always a good idea to test the speed by asking someone to view the presentation. A common mistake is to change the display before people have had a chance to read the information.

If a speaker is giving the presentation, it might be better to let them choose manually when to move to the next display. This can be done with a mouse click or by using a hand-held control.

One benefit of using presentation software is that it is easy to edit the presentation. Slides can be added or removed, the order of slides can be changed or information on a slide can be amended.

Rules for effective presentations

- Keep the information simple – the speaker should be able to expand on the information on display.
- Use opening and closing slides to set the scene and emphasise the important points.
- Avoid using too many slides – each slide should be displayed for between one and two minutes.
- Avoid putting too much information on each slide. Use bullet points – no more than four or five per slide.

Website design

Websites are a way of presenting information to viewers using the world wide web (Unit 4). When using multimedia software to design websites, most of the same rules apply as for designing presentations – except that a speaker will not be present, and different pages can be connected in various ways using hyperlinks.

You can think of a website as a series of interlocking pieces (or web pages) of information. This is different to the way information is displayed in a presentation, where you start at the beginning and sequentially work your way to the end.

A presentation is made up of a linear sequence of slides, while a website consists of several web pages interconnected in different ways

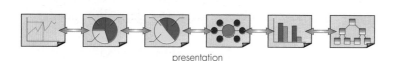

presentation

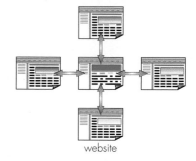

website

Main features of websites	Business examples
Web pages – these can display text and images.	Businesses can include text and photographs of their products.
Embedded files – these are animated images and sound files to which links can be made from the web pages.	On-line music stores can let customers hear a short extract from a song before they make a purchase.
Hyperlinks – these are links to other web pages within the website or elsewhere on the world wide web.	Links can be made to pages providing technical information about the product. Only those people interested in this need to see it.
Drop-down menus – these work like the menu bar on most computer software. Selecting the drop-down menu reveals a list of options from which to make a choice.	On-line computer stores can ask customers to choose from a list of add-on software bundles.
Web forms – these enable the website to collect information from the user. They work just like the data capture form on a database (Unit 3)	Customers complete an on-line order form in order to make a purchase.
Counters – these display how many visitors have viewed the website. Most counters work by depositing **cookies** onto the visitor's computer.	Businesses can display how popular their website has been. This can give the website extra credibility with visitors.
Cookies – small text files placed by the website onto the user's computer. These help the website recognise users when they next visit the site.	Websites can customise their appearance for individual users. For example, on-line bookshops can display on their homepage special offers in the customer's favourite category of books.

In order to design a website, you need to carry out the following tasks.

1 Decide what information you want to display.
2 Produce a 'map' of the website showing what information is to be displayed, where it will be found, and how hyperlinks will connect the different parts of the website.
3 Sketch out each page.
4 Produce the pages.

Most publishing software can be used to create simple web pages containing hyperlinks. Each page needs to be saved as an **HTML** file before it can be viewed on a web browser. HTML stands for hypertext mark-up language. This is the computer language which allows computers to understand the data contained in a web page. Web-authoring software enables more sophisticated websites to be built and converted into HTML.

Rules for effective web design

■ Keep the information on each page simple. Complex information and lots of images take a long time to download from the internet.
■ Keep the basic design of each page the same – for example, the layout and background should be similar on each page. This helps people navigate their way through your website.
■ Keep the number of hyperlinks needed to reach each piece of information to a minimum. Ideally it should be possible to reach any point on the website using less than five hyperlinks.
■ Make it simple to update the site.

It is vital that businesses have well-designed websites. The internet is a highly competitive place. Anyone can set up a website and begin trading. Often the only thing that can give a firm an edge over its competitors is the quality of its website.

6

CAD/CAM and image-creation software

CAD and CAM

Computer-aided design (**CAD**) is a system used to create a computer-drawn design of an artefact.

Computer-aided manufacture (**CAM**) is a system used to control the operation of production equipment. This enables high quality standardised products to be made.

The two systems are often linked together. CAD produces the design and CAM manufactures the final product.

Benefits of CAD software

The main benefits to a business of using CAD software are as follows.

- Designs can be drawn much more quickly and accurately than by hand.
- Designs can be edited and manipulated quickly.
- Drawings can be rotated and resized. This enables the design to be viewed from different angles and distances.
- Designs can be saved and re-used to help produce future designs.
- Designs can be sent to a client very quickly as an e-mail attachment.

Designs made using CAD software can be 'rotated' in virtual space, and seen from every angle

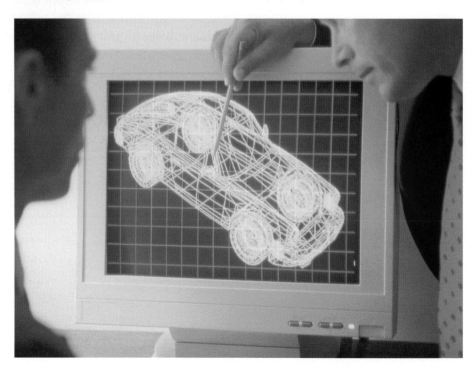

Advanced CAD software may also have the following features.

■ Some CAD software can calculate the cost of an artefact based on the components specified in the design. The effect that changing the design makes to the final cost can then be calculated.
■ Some software can suggest suitable materials and design features for the artefact. For example, it could suggest that a roof of a certain size must have supporting walls of a particular strength.
■ Some software can simulate the performance of the artefact under certain environmental conditions – for example, to test whether a building could withstand a hurricane.

Benefits of CAM software

CAM software controls the operations of manufacturing equipment. The benefits to a business of using CAM software include those below.

■ When shapes need to be cut from a sheet of material, CAM software can organise how to cut the maximum number of pieces with the minimum waste, taking into account the properties of the material (such as the weave and pattern of fabric, for example).
■ CAM software can specify the size and depth of holes to be drilled, and ensure that all holes are cut to within a specified tolerance level.
■ CAM software can specify the speed of production – for example, the number of holes that can be drilled in one minute.
■ CAM software can specify the order of machine processes, to ensure, for example, that certain pieces are cut before others, or that pilot holes are drilled before the final hole size.
■ CAM software means that a range of processes can be carried out one after the other with no need for intervention from the operator. For example, chess pieces can be machined from blanks of material.
■ CAM software means that machines can work at much higher speeds than when there is manual intervention.

Automated manufacture, under the control of CAM software

Image-creation software

Images

An image is simply any non-text-based information. Examples include photographs, clip-art, movies and images created by the user.

It is important to know about the different types of image files and their properties. Some software, such as web browsers, will only allow certain types of image file to be displayed on the screen or printed. There are two main forms of image file.

- **Bitmap files** store the picture as individual dots or bits of data. Each dot represents one piece of data about the picture. From a distance, the dots seem to merge into one single image. Each dot is called a **pixel**. The more pixels in a picture, the greater its resolution. High-resolution bitmap images look much clearer and more realistic than low-resolution pictures. The big problem with bitmap files is that they use a large amount of computer memory.
- **Vector-based files** store the picture as a series of equations and other data. For example, if the picture contains a circle, the circle is stored using data that describes its shape and size. As a result much less memory is needed to store a vector-based image than a bitmap image.

A bitmap image

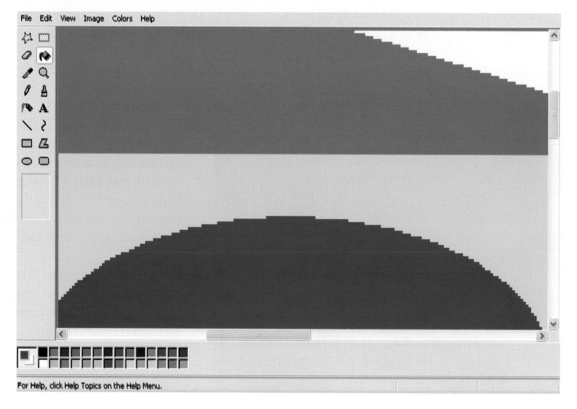

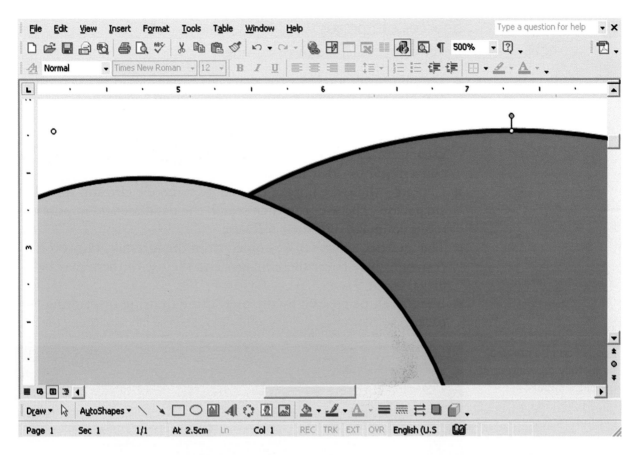

A vector-based image

The main image file types and their properties are given in the table below.

Image file type	Properties
BMP (Bitmap)	Data is stored as individual bits, which together form a map of the whole image
JPEG (Joint Photograph Experts' Group)	Data is stored in a similar way to bitmaps. JPEG files can be viewed using a web browser. Most image files can be converted into JPEG format.
GIF (graphics interchange format)	Stores images limited to 256 standard colours. GIF files can be viewed using a web browser but are less detailed than JPEG images. This is a compressed bitmap file.
AI (Adobe Illustrator)	Data is stored as a series of mathematical equations. Because of this you can enlarge vector images without loss of quality. This is an example of a vector-based file.

Sources of images

Image sources include the following.

- Digital camera images – these are already stored in JPEG format and can be manipulated using photo-editing software.
- Photographic prints and drawings – these have to be converted from printed output into a digital file using a scanner. Scanners usually create them as bitmap files but they can then be converted into other formats.
- Clip-art – these are images created by someone else and stored in a database. The user can then search the database and import the required image into their software.
- The internet – files can be copied from the internet. However, copyright may cover these images and the use of them may be illegal (Unit 9).
- Images can be created by the user, using drawing or painting packages.

Images can be created by literally drawing on a graphics tablet

Drawing and painting packages

Drawing packages usually create vector-based images and painting software usually creates bitmap images. Whichever type of software is used, the same basic functions can be found, as described below.

- Layering – an image can be built up as a series of layers. The sequence of layers can be altered. A company could use layers to place its company name onto an image of one of its products.
- Copying and pasting – different sections of the image can be copied and pasted to create a different image.
- Filling an object – for example, a circle can be 'filled' with colour to create a solid shape.
- Adding filters and textures to change the appearance of the image – for example, shadows can be added to make the object appear three-dimensional.
- Changing object colours – for example, a red object can be turned into any different colour or shade. Most packages allow you to mix different colours together to create very specific colour styles.
- Creating animation effects – for example, some software will allow the user to create copies of an original image and then adapt subsequent versions. The images can then be viewed one after the other very quickly. This turns them into a very simple animation. When stored as GIF files, they can liven up a web page.

Section 1 Summary questions

Work through these questions to check your knowledge of each unit.

■ 1 Publishing software

1 Explain the difference between word-processors and desktop publishing software.

2 Explain three benefits to businesses of using publishing software.

3 Explain the difference between the 'copy and paste' function and the 'cut and paste' function.

4 A business wishes to use 'mail-merge' to send personalised letters to a group of customers. Describe how the business would do this.

5 **a)** Explain the difference between the 'spell check' facility and the 'grammar check' facility.
   b) Explain why the 'spell check' facility would not be able to correct the following sentence: 'I here that their is a problem with hour currant advertising campaign.'

■ 2 Spreadsheets

1 Each spreadsheet is made up of a number of different cells. Explain where on a spreadsheet you could find cell B6.

2 What different types of input data can be entered into a cell?

3 **a)** Shreena wants to enter the price of a bag of crisps into cell B6. She types in 0.4. The spreadsheet displays this as £0.40. Explain how cell B6 has been formatted to make this happen.
   b) Shreena wishes to display a number in cell B7 that equals the price of the bag of crisps multiplied by ten. Write out the formula that can make this happen.
   c) Shreena wishes to put the same formula into cells B8 to B20. Explain how she can do this quickly.
   d) Shreena puts the following formula into cell H2: H2 = If(C5<50,'Buy more stock','You have enough stock'). Explain carefully what information will be displayed in cell H2.

4 List four pieces of information that should be added to a bar graph to make it easier for someone to read.

5 Andy runs a painting and decorating business. He wants to build a spreadsheet model so he can work out the costs of decorating a house. He knows that each square metre (m^2) of wall will cost 50p to paint. In addition, his wages work out at 30p for each square metre (m^2) of wall. Describe how the computer model would work.

6 Explain how a computer model can be used to carry out 'what-if analysis'.

■ 3 Databases

1 Explain the difference between a spreadsheet and a database.

2 List three benefits to a business of using a computerised database.

3 What is the difference between a database 'field' and a database 'record'?

4 Why is it important that each database file has a key field?

5 What is the difference between a flat-file database and a relational database?

6 A doctor's surgery wishes to set up a patient database. Briefly describe the main steps needed to create the database.

7 An estate agent uses a database to store details of properties for sale.
   a) Explain the search criteria that could be used to find all three-bedroom properties in the database.
   b) Explain the search criteria that could be used to find all three-bedroom properties whose selling price is below £120,000.
   c) The estate agent wishes to produce a report displaying all the properties for sale with the cheapest at the top of the list and the most expensive at the end. Explain how this could be done.

■ 4 Communications software

1 What hardware and software is needed to connect a personal computer (PC) to the internet?

2 What are the two main parts of the internet?

3 Mandy wishes to search for the website of a business located in the United Kingdom. She knows the name of the business. Describe two different ways that Mandy could try to locate the firm on the internet.

4 Identify four benefits to businesses of having a website.

5 Mandy wishes to send a copy of a spreadsheet to a customer. She decides to use e-mail. Describe the steps needed to send the file.

6 Mandy receives an e-mail from an unknown person. The e-mail contains an attachment. What should Mandy do?

7 Explain what video-conferencing is. What benefits can it bring to businesses that use it?

■ 5 Multimedia

1 Explain three ways that using presentation software can improve the quality of a presentation.

2 Brian is the sales manager for an internet bookstore. He has been asked to produce a presentation outlining the sales figures for the past six months. Brian decides to produce two versions of the presentation. One is to be presented by a speaker and the other is to be put onto a computer network for people to view without an accompanying speaker. Explain three ways in which the two versions of the same presentation might be different.

3 Explain the following features of a website.
   a) hyperlink
   b) web form
   c) counter

4 A book shop wishes to set up a website where customers can buy books over the internet. Describe the main features of the website and how the book shop can use the website to provide a personal service for its customers.

5 Phil wishes to produce a website for his second-hand car business. He asks you for some advice. Give Phil three tips on how to produce a good website.

6 What do the initials HTML stand for? What is HTML?

■ 6 CAD/CAM and image-creation software

1 What do the initials CAD and CAM stand for? Explain the difference between them.

2 Describe three features of CAD software.

3 Explain three benefits to a business of using CAD software.

4 Explain two benefits of using CAM.

5 Explain the difference between a bitmap image and a vector-based image.

6 Which type of image file usually takes up more computer memory, a bitmap image or a vector-based image?

7 Jason takes some photographs of his firm's products using a digital camera. Give the name of the image file type used to store the photograph.

8 Jason wishes to put an old photographic print of himself onto his business's website. Explain how he can do this.

9 Describe four features that can be found on most types of image-creation software.

Section 2

Business and its environment

7

Objectives of business

Objectives

All businesses have to have objectives. An **objective** is something that the owners of the business want it to achieve.

For most businesses the main objective is to make as much profit as possible. **Profit** is simply the difference between the income the firm receives from selling its products and the cost of running the business.

Profit is needed to reward the owners of the business who have invested their own **capital** into the firm. If the firm doesn't make enough profit the owners might remove their capital and invest it elsewhere. If this happens the business might have to cease trading.

Each firm may have other, secondary objectives. These are often to do with how the firm intends to make a profit. Other objectives might be:

■ to make a high quality product
■ to have satisfied customers
■ to be the biggest firm in the market
■ to be the fastest growing firm in the market
■ to produce its products in an environmentally friendly way.

Sometimes these objectives might be in conflict with each other, or with the need to make a profit. For example, high quality products might be expensive to produce. This will increase the firm's costs. Unless it can persuade the customer to pay a higher price for the product it will earn less profit.

All firms need to decide which priorities are most important. They also need to decide how best to achieve the objectives.

You might have your own objectives for the next couple of years. One might be to get the highest possible GCSE grades. Another might be to play a musical instrument or be the captain of a sports team. These objectives might conflict with each other. For example, studying for GCSEs takes a lot of time – so does practising a musical instrument or training for a sports team. You might therefore need to compromise or even give up on a particular objective.

Stakeholders

Businesses also have to satisfy a number of different stakeholders. A **stakeholder** is anyone who is affected by the actions of the firm. The main stakeholders and their interests in a firm are given in the table below.

Stakeholder	Main interest
Owners	Will the firm make as much profit as possible now and in the future?
Employees	Will the firm pay decent wages and provide good working conditions?
Suppliers	Will the firm pay its bills on time?
Customers	Will the firm produce high quality goods that offer good value for money?
Local residents	Will the firm affect my quality of life – for example, by polluting the local environment?
Competitors	Will the firm be too successful and put me out of business?
Government	Will the firm prosper and grow, providing jobs for people and paying taxes to us?

Sometimes these interests will be in conflict with each other. For example, the employees' desire for decent wages and working conditions may be in conflict with the owners' desire for large profits. This is because higher wages mean increased costs, but consumers may not be prepared to pay higher prices unless the quality of the product can be improved.

It is ultimately up to the owners of the business to resolve any conflict between the company objectives, the stakeholder interests and the main objective of making a profit. Large businesses often delegate responsibility for making these decisions to senior managers. But these managers are accountable to the owners. If they don't like the decisions made by the management, the owners can replace them with other people.

Measurable objectives

Objectives are important when a business takes on any new system or equipment. The company should have objectives based on the benefits that it expects the new system to bring. For example, a firm might install a new computer system, with the objective of reducing the time spent on routine administration by 10%. The administration time must be measured, both before and after the installation, to see if the objective has been achieved.

■ ICT Case study

Belmont Estate Agents is a small estate agency business. The business has three branches in the towns of Market Harrington and Great Snittering. The business has seen rapid growth in the past three years as both towns are expanding in size. This is due to a recently opened high-speed train line into London, which has attracted a large number of commuters into the area.

The main objective of the business is to achieve high profits for its three owners. In 2000–2001, the business earned a total profit of £85,000. The business intends profits to increase by at least 10% every year for the next five years.

As well as this main objective, the business has a number of secondary objectives. These are all intended to help the business achieve its main aim of making high profits. The secondary objectives are:

■ to increase the number of properties available for sale by 10% each year for the next three years
■ to offer the most competitive service to people selling their properties in the two towns
■ to reduce the time it takes to sell a property from an average of ten weeks to an average of six weeks.

As a way of achieving these objectives, Belmont Estate Agents has decided to set up its own website. Properties for sale will be advertised on-line and the owners hope that this will help to make the business more attractive for both buyers and sellers.

In order to set up the website, the agency needs to store all of its property details electronically. As a result its present computer system will need to be upgraded and all staff issued with digital cameras. The owners estimate that the new computer system will cost in the region of £30,000. In addition, the owners anticipate that introducing the new system will cause some disruption to the business. They conclude that the costs of introducing and operating the new website and computer system will reduce the profits in the current year, but that this should be more than made up for in higher profits in the future.

Tasks

1 Explain the main aim of the business.
2 Explain how the secondary objectives are expected to help the business achieve its main objective.
3 Describe how the new website might make the business more attractive for both house buyers and house sellers.
4 Describe what 'disruption' and 'higher costs' might result from introducing the new website and computer system.
5 Explain how the introduction of the computer system might be in conflict with the main aim of the business.
6 Explain how introducing a website might help the business achieve its objectives.

8 | External constraints on business activity: the market

Most businesses in the UK aim to make a profit. They do this by buying in resources, which are then used to make products. These products are then sold to the firm's customers. The firm will make a profit if the income it receives from its customers is greater than the cost of running the business.

Essentially, all businesses aim to make profit by selling products to customers

Most firms in the UK also face competition from other firms. These other firms are often trying to sell very similar products to the same customers. These firms are said to be in **competition** with each other. They are competing for the customers' money. The most successful firms are the ones who produce the products that customers want to buy – the products for which there is **consumer demand**.

Consumer demand

There are many factors that help influence the level of consumer demand. Some of the most important ones are described below.

Price

Consumers generally prefer products that are sold at lower prices. Often the easiest way for a firm to increase the number of sales is to reduce its prices. There are some exceptions to this. Sometimes consumers use the price of a product as an indication of its value for money. If the product is sold too cheaply consumers may be reluctant to buy it because they think its quality is poor. A good example of such a product is perfume.

Quality of the product

If two identical products have the same price, consumers would generally buy the higher quality one. Most consumers want affordable products that offer good value for money.

Image

Some products have a particular image with which consumers want to be associated. Products that have a strong **brand** image include some soft drinks and clothing. One way to create a strong brand image is to spend large sums of money on advertising the product.

Income

An increase or decrease in income will change the kinds of products that consumers want to buy. Products that people generally buy more of when they become richer are known as 'luxuries'. Examples include sports cars and restaurant meals. Products that people generally buy less of as they get richer are known as 'inferior goods'. Examples include white bread and bus travel.

Competitors

Competitors will also be a major influence affecting the level of consumer demand for a particular firm's product.

Competition

Generally speaking, a market will be highly competitive if the following conditions are met.

■ There are a large number of equal-sized firms. This means that customers should have a lot of choice over which firm's products they buy.
■ Firms produce identical products. This means firms can't use advertising to convince the consumer that their product is better than their competitor's (and so worth paying more for). It also means that consumers won't buy a firm's product if it is more expensive than the prices charged by its competitors.
■ Consumers have good information about the products for sale. This is important. It means that consumers know the prices charged by all the firms. This enables them to buy from the cheapest supplier. Some people argue that the internet is helping to make markets more competitive. This is because it makes it easier for consumers to compare prices.
■ It is easy for new firms to enter the market and compete with the existing firms. Some markets are difficult to enter because they have 'barriers to entry'. A good example is car manufacturing. Very few firms can afford to build the huge car factories that are needed to mass-produce large numbers of cars. Producing cars on a small scale is not competitive because of the very high fixed costs involved (Unit 18).

Competition and the internet

Markets where firms face little competition are called monopoly markets and the firms in them are known as **monopolies**. Generally speaking, monopoly markets are good for the owners of the firms in the market, but bad for consumers and potential competitors.
It can be argued that the increased use of the internet by businesses and consumers has helped to make markets more competitive. This has happened for a number of reasons.

1 The internet has enabled many more firms to set up in business. The costs of doing business on the internet are much cheaper – for example, firms do not need to have retail outlets, as they can sell directly into people's homes. This means that the internet has reduced barriers to entry.

2 The internet makes it possible for small firms to reach a global market. Consequently, there has been a growth in the number of small specialist manufacturers and retailers, who can sell their products anywhere in the world via the internet. One example in the UK is that of a specialist sausage producing company, which takes orders on its website and then posts the products to customers.

3 The internet makes it easier for consumers to compare prices. From a computer, a customer can load the websites of a number of different retailers and compare the prices of the products. This might take days if the customer had to go round the shops on foot or by car. There are also a number of internet sites that will make the price comparisons for you. The customer can then compare the prices and make a purchase from the best supplier.

The internet means that even the smallest company can now access the global market

■ *ICT Activity*

Chumpo Chocolates PLC manufacture and sell a range of chocolate bars and other snacks. Their main market is the UK. The following table gives details on Chumpo Chocolate's sales over a ten-year period.

Year	1993	1994	1995	1996	1997	1998	1999	2000	2001	2002
Sales (£m)	95.3	95.7	95.6	97.1	97.2	96.9	96.4	92.7	90.4	88.5

Tasks

1 Enter the above information onto a spreadsheet.
2 Create a graph to illustrate Chumpo Chocolate's sales figures for the ten-year period.
3 Using a word-processing package, write a short report describing the trend in sales.
4 Suggest some possible reasons for the trends and make some suggestions as to what the business could do to improve sales from 2003 onwards.
5 Include a copy of the graph in your report.

9 External constraints on business activity: the law

There are many laws that set out how firms should operate, and these have important influences on the behaviour of businesses. In this unit, we will look at three important areas: consumer protection, the use of ICT and health and safety.

Companies must operate within the law

Since 1973, the UK has been a member of the European Union (EU). The EU aims to harmonise laws throughout its member countries. In other words, within its membership, the EU doesn't want some firms to have an unfair advantage over their competitors because they operate in a country with fewer rules and regulations. The EU issues **directives** that then require member countries to change existing laws or introduce new ones. A number of the new laws that have come into being in the UK since 1973 have been as a result of EU directives.

Consumer protection legislation

Trade Descriptions Act 1968

This law makes it illegal for a retailer to give a false or misleading description of a product offered for sale. For example, a piece of jewellery described as a '24-carat diamond ring' *must* contain a 24-carat diamond.

Consumer Credit Act 1974

Sometimes people take out loans in order to buy expensive products such as cars and computers. The Consumer Credit Act gives consumers a 14-day cooling-off period after signing the credit agreement. During this period, consumers are allowed to change their mind and cancel the agreement.

Weights and Measures Act 1979

This law makes it illegal for retailers to sell products that contain less than the amount described on the packaging. For example, a one-litre carton of milk *must* contain at least one litre of milk and a five-kilogram bag of potatoes must weigh at least five kilograms.

As a result of EU directives, all goods sold by weight or volume must now display this information in metric units (kilograms and litres) rather than imperial units (pounds and ounces and pints).

Sale of Goods Act 1979

This law says that all goods sold must meet three criteria.

1 The goods should be fit for their purpose. In other words, a product should do the job that it is supposed to. For example, a portable CD player should be able to play CDs without constantly jumping.
2 The goods should be of merchantable quality. This means that the product should be made to a standard that enables it to perform the task for which it was designed. For example, all the components of the CD player should work.
3 The product should perform as it is described. For example, a CD player described as having an anti-shock device should contain an anti-shock device.

The law says that if goods fail to meet any of these criteria, the consumer is entitled to a full refund from the retailer who sold the goods.

Supply of Goods and Services Act 1982

This law extended the Sale of Goods Act to services. For example, a painter and decorator must provide a service that matches the description of the service offered to the customer at the outset, and the work must be of a reasonable standard.

Consumer Protection Act 1987

This law was introduced following an EU directive. It extended the Sale of Goods Act and the Supply of Goods and Services Act to make sure that firms are liable for any problems that their below-standard products cause to consumers.

For example, a washing machine might leak because of poor design or installation and flood a house. If it could be proved that the flood occurred because of a faulty product, the firm that supplied that product would have to pay compensation to the consumer for the damage caused by the flood.

Computer legislation

Data Protection Act 1984, 1988

The Data Protection Act was first introduced in 1984. It was then amended in 1988 to comply with an EU directive.

The law is designed to protect the privacy of people who have personal data stored on the computers of other organisations. The law places restrictions on what data can be held and what organisations can do with it. The law gives individuals the right to see their data and request that it is deleted if the data does not comply with the law.

Someone who has personal data stored about them is called a **data-subject**. Each organisation is required to have a data controller whose job is to make sure that the organisation complies with the law.

The Data Protection Act lists eight principles that the organisation should follow.

1 Personal data shall not be stored or processed unless the data-subject has given their permission or the processing is necessary.
2 Personal data should only be used for the purpose for which it was originally collected.
3 Only data that is directly relevant to the needs of the task shall be collected.
4 The data must be accurate and be kept up to date.
5 The data must only be stored for as long as is necessary to carry out the task for which it was originally collected.

6 The data must be processed in ways that meet the rights of the data-subjects (see below).
7 The organisation should ensure that the data is kept secure and is not copied and used without authorisation.
8 The organisation must not transfer the data to organisations outside the EU. The only exceptions are if the other country is able to ensure that the rights of the data-subjects can be met.

There are a number of exemptions to the Act. An organisation does not need to follow these eight principles if:

■ the data is kept for personal use
■ the data is used for the calculation of wages and other payroll information
■ the data is held for reasons of national security
■ the data is on a mailing list and the data-subject has given his or her permission.

Data-subjects have a number of rights under the act.

■ They have a right to see a copy of all the personal data stored by an organisation.
■ They can request that inaccurate information is amended and data that does not meet the eight principles is deleted.

These rights do not apply to police intelligence data or to tax records.

Copyright, Designs and Patents Act 1988

This law makes it illegal to copy any computer file without permission from the copyright owner. Anyone who breaks this law can face an unlimited fine. Examples of breaking this law include:

■ copying text or an image from the internet and then re-using it without permission – for example, copying a company logo
■ copying a computer program used at work or school and running it on a computer at home
■ using software without a proper licence – for example, using an **evaluation package** after the trial period has ended.

Computer Misuse Act 1990

This law was designed to prevent people gaining unauthorised access to computer systems and causing damage. Anyone found guilty can face an unlimited fine and up to five years in prison. Examples of how this law can be broken include:

■ hacking into a computer system; copying, editing or deleting files
■ deliberately planting computer viruses into computer systems through e-mail attachments, for example.

Health and safety

There are a number of laws that govern the safe use of computers. Computers are pieces of electrical equipment that people can use continuously for long periods. As a result, there are health risks from using them. These laws place restrictions on how employers can organise their workforce.

There are some basic health and safety risks associated with using ICT in the workplace

Health and Safety at Work Act 1974

This law places a general requirement for all employers to take reasonable steps to protect the health and safety of their employees. Equally, the Act requires employees to take care over their own health and safety and that of their work colleagues.

For example, you might spot that a computer cable is trailed across a floor and it might cause someone to trip over it. The law says that you are under an obligation to tell people and try and have the hazard removed. This applies whether you are the employer or an employee.

Health and Safety (Display Screen Equipment) Regulations 1992

These regulations apply to the use of computer workstations in business organisations. They were introduced following an EU directive. The regulations require employers to do five main things. They must:

1 assess the health and safety risks that might result from using their computers
2 ensure that their computer equipment meets minimum safety standards
3 plan workers' activities so that they can take regular breaks away from their computer
4 provide eye-tests to staff who regularly use visual display units (monitors) as part of their job
5 provide information and training on how workers can take their own actions to minimise health and safety risks.

Health and safety risks	Action to reduce risk
Eye-strain from staring at a monitor	Use large monitors
	Fit a screen-filter to reduce the glare from the screen
	Ensure the work area is well lit
	Take regular breaks
Repetitive strain injury (RSI) from over-use of a **keyboard** or mouse	Use an ergonomically designed keyboard
	Take regular breaks
	Do finger stretching exercises
Back-strain	Use a proper computer chair
	Sit at the computer with a good body posture
	Take regular breaks, walk and exercise the back muscles

It's important to adopt the right posture when sitting at a workstation, to avoid back-strain

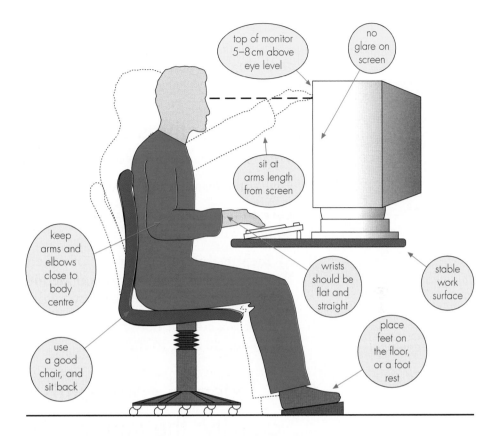

top of monitor 5–8 cm above eye level

no glare on screen

sit at arms length from screen

keep arms and elbows close to body centre

wrists should be flat and straight

stable work surface

use a good chair, and sit back

place feet on the floor, or a foot rest

■ *ICT Activity*

You have been asked by the personnel department of Sprights Bank to design a series of leaflets. The leaflets are for the bank's employees who regularly use computer equipment. The leaflets will be displayed in all work areas.

The leaflets should cover the following areas:

- how computers can be a potential health and safety hazard
- what the employer and each employee can do to minimise these risks.

The leaflets should be well designed and eye-catching. They should present the information clearly and concisely. Appropriate use of pictures and text formatting could help achieve this.

Section 2 Summary questions

Work through these questions to check your knowledge of each unit.

■ 7 Objectives of business

1 What is the main objective of most firms?

2 Give three examples of other objectives.

3 Give an example of two objectives that might sometimes be in conflict with each other.

4 a) Identify four different types of stakeholder for a supermarket.
   b) For each stakeholder that you identified, explain one aspect of the firm's performance they might be very interested in.

5 If there is a conflict between a firm's objectives, who ultimately has to decide what to do?

■ 8 External constraints on business activity: the market

1 Explain three things that most consumers will take into account before deciding which products to buy.

2 Explain what is meant by the term 'inferior goods' and give an example.

3 Explain what is meant by the term 'luxury goods' and give an example.

4 What is meant by the phrase 'high barriers to entry'? How does this help to make a market less competitive than one with low barriers to entry?

5 Apart from barriers to entry, explain two other factors that help influence the amount of competition in a market.

6 Who would usually prefer a market to be dominated by a monopoly – a consumer or a business owner? Explain your answer.

7 Explain how the internet is helping to make firms more competitive.

■ 9 External constraints on business activity: the law

1   A pair of shoes is advertised as being made from leather. In fact, the shoes are made of plastic. Which consumer protection law has been broken?

2   Desperate Dan buys a cow pie advertised as weighing five kilograms when in fact it only weighs four and a half kilograms. Which consumer protection law has been broken?

3   As a result of buying a faulty video player, Mr Jackson's prize videotape of Dad's Army has been ruined. Under which law is he entitled to ask the manufacturer and retailer for a replacement videotape?

4   The Data Protection Act is designed to protect the rights of all 'data-subjects'. Who or what is a data-subject?

5   **a)** Give four of the key principles of the Data Protection Act.
    b) Under what circumstances might an organisation's computer data not be covered by the Act?

6   BLSBC Bank uses an image on its website that was copied from the website of Haloyds Bank. Haloyds Bank did not give permission for the image to be used. Which law has been broken?

7   Describe two actions that employers must take in order to comply with the Health and Safety (Display Screen Equipment) Regulations 1992.

8   Give three health problems that might result from using a computer for a long period of time. For each, identify one way in which the risk of a problem could be reduced.

Section 3

Human resources

10 HR functions: job roles and working conditions

The most important resource employed by most business organisations is the people. These people are known as personnel, or **employees**. In this unit, we will look at the main job roles carried out by people at work. We will also see how new technology is changing the way that most people work.

Job roles

There are four main job roles within any business.

1 **Directors** are the people appointed by the owners to run the whole business on their behalf. The directors are responsible for making sure that the business objectives of the owners are met. The directors also have a legal responsibility for things such as workplace health and safety. The most important director is usually known as the managing director. He or she is responsible for deciding what the other directors do.
2 **Managers** have the job of implementing the decisions made by the directors. They are responsible for planning, controlling and co-ordinating the day-to-day operations of the business. They are also responsible for motivating the employees that they manage.
3 **Supervisors** are people who make sure that a group of workers carry out the jobs that they are employed to do. A supervisor usually reports to a manager.
4 **Operatives** are the people who carry out the specific tasks needed to perform a job.

For example, the directors of a telesales organisation, in considering the strategic direction of the company, may decide that the business needs to introduce a fully computerised telephone system. The managers in the company would then decide which system to buy, how to implement it and how to train the staff. Once the system was installed, the supervisors would make sure that the operatives knew how to use the new system properly and worked as efficiently as possible.

The operatives work in the open-plan area of this office, while their supervisor works close by in a partitioned section

How ICT is changing working conditions

ICT is a constant influence on the ways in which people work. As new technologies are introduced, workplaces adapt to them. A good example is the increased use of e-mail and text-messaging.

Teleworking

It is possible to work from home or a work-centre and communicate with the business using internet technology. This is known as **teleworking**. For example, a person who writes sales brochures could create them on a home computer and send them via e-mail to the employer. In the same way, the employer could send the person files to work on. Any job that can be done on a computer at work can be done on a computer at home.

One benefit of teleworking is that people don't need to spend time commuting to work. Another is that people can work flexibly – they don't necessarily have to work within strict office hours, which can make it easier to combine work with bringing up a family. Problems with teleworking include the lack of contact with work colleagues and the feeling of isolation.

Hotdesking

Traditionally, office employees stored their work-related documents in large filing cabinets and, for practical reasons, they had to work at a desk located close to the files that they needed.

Modern workplaces store most of the information on a computer network. This means that people can work wherever they have access to the network. As a result, people no longer have to have their own individual office space and desk.

Hotdesking is the term used to describe a situation where people work wherever they can find a space. Businesses like it because it can mean fewer desks are needed – at any one time some staff will be out of the office or on holiday. This helps to reduce costs. A problem is that some staff find not having their own personal space at work very stressful and de-motivating.

Monitoring performance

ICT can be used to measure the performance of employees in great detail, allowing it to be monitored over time. For example, in telephone call centres the computer system can record how many telephone calls each operative takes in an hour and how long each call lasts. This can help managers to set targets for the operatives to work more productively. Some people claim that this pressure can be de-motivating for staff.

Many companies make use of call centres to keep in touch with current customers, and to find new ones

■ ICT Activity

The following data was collected by the human resources department at a telephone call centre. The computer recorded the length and number of telephone calls received by each operator.

Name of operator	Number of calls received	Average length of call (minutes)	Total time spent on calls (minutes)	Time at work (hours)	Time at work (minutes)	Percentage of work-time spent on calls
Brian	152	2		8		
Mandy	145	2.5		8		
Punita	202	1.5		6		
Fred	154	2		8		
Liam	171	2		8		
Mary	178	3		10		
Anuj	113	3		8		
Warren	140	2		8		
Francisca	137	3		8		
Tom	167	2		8		

Tasks

1 Enter the above data into a spreadsheet. Use appropriate formulas to calculate the information needed for the three blank columns.

2 Who is the best worker? Give reasons for your answer. Does everyone in your group agree? If not why not?

11 HR functions: recruitment

One of the most important jobs of the human resources, or personnel, department is to **recruit** new staff. If a firm appoints the wrong person for a job, it can be very difficult to replace them with someone else.

The recruitment process

There are a number of stages in the recruitment process.

1 Job analysis

The firm needs to identify exactly what the job involves. This could be done by talking with managers or observing how existing staff perform the job.

2 Job description

This is a description of all the main tasks that the job will require the person to perform. It is based on the job analysis already carried out.

3 Person specification

This is a description of the ideal person needed to perform the job. It will be a list of their personal characteristics – such as temperament and personality – as well as their skills, qualifications and experience.

There are number of things that cannot be included in the person specification. These include the person's age, gender and ethnic group, and disabilities. Including these would be illegal under anti-discrimination laws such as the Race Relations Act.

4 Advertisement of the vacancy

The same principles apply to advertising a job as to advertising a product. The advertisement should be carefully designed and put in places where it will be seen by people likely to be interested.

Most firms will produce a draft of a job advertisement using publishing software

---

Wanted: Telephone Sales Executive

The *Midgeley Advertiser* is Midgeley's leading independent evening newspaper. We currently have a vacancy for a Telephone Sales Executive to work in our busy sales office.

Main duties: Receiving telephone orders for classified advertising space
                           Processing telephone orders

Responsible to: Classified Sales Manager

Hours: Monday to Friday, 8.30 am to 5.00 pm

You should be hard-working and organised with a fun personality. Experience of working in a sales office would be an advantage.

The *Midgeley Advertiser* offers a competitive salary and a subsidised staff canteen.

If you wish to apply please send your current CV and a covering letter to:

     Mrs J. Stammers
     Personnel Department
     Midgeley Newspapers Ltd.
     21 Shorts Road
     Midgeley
     M1 E17

Closing date for applications is Friday 15 March.

The Midgeley Advertiser is an equal opportunities employer.

The firm has the option of advertising the vacancy to existing employees (called internal recruitment), or to people outside the business (called external recruitment). Most firms will use both.

The firm can also approach specialist agencies. These will store information about people interested in particular types of jobs. The agency can then recommend the most suitable people to the business.

Some benefits and problems associated with advertising in different places are outlined in the table on page 76.

Place where job is advertised	Benefits	Problems
Internal notice boards and newsletters	Seen by existing staff who know the organisation	These staff will need replacing in their old job
Careers service	Has a large number of school-leavers on its database	The careers service, not the business, decides who will be interviewed
Job centres	Large number of unemployed people on their database	The job centre, not the business, decides who will be interviewed
Agencies	Large number of specialist staff on their database	The agency, not the business, decides who will be interviewed
Internet	Huge numbers of people may see the advertisement Cheaper than other advertising media	People who are not really qualified may be tempted to apply
Specialist publications	People already working in a similar type of job will see the advertisement	It will only be seen by people already working in that type of job
Local newspapers	People living in the area will see the advertisement Relatively cheap	Not seen by people outside the area
National newspapers	Large number of people across the whole country will see the advertisement	Very expensive

5 Receipt of applications

Most firms will want to see a completed application form or the person's **Curriculum Vitae** (CV). This enables them to see if the person has the skills and qualifications needed to do the job. Most candidates will produce their letter and CV using a word-processor. This is because the documents will look neater and more professional. However, some firms might insist that the letter be hand-written. This is because they will still expect staff to hand-write documents at some stage. They may also wish to use a graphologist whose study of a sample of the hand-writing could contribute to a personality profile of the writer.

6 Interviewing of candidates

An interview gives the business the chance to talk with the candidate and find out more about their skills and their personality. ICT can help here – for example, the business could ask candidates to take a computer-based **psychometric test**. These are tests that are designed to find out about the person's personality and ability to handle pressure.

At an interview, both candidate and employer get a chance to find out if the person is right for the job

7 Selection of the right person for the job

After the interview, the firm should be able to see which applicant has the right qualities, skills and experience to be able to do the job. That person will be the right person for the job.

■ *ICT Activity 1*

You have been asked by your school to produce a set of documents to help recruit a new teacher. The documents you need to produce are:

■ a job description
■ a person specification
■ an advertisement for the job
■ a checklist of interview questions.

Tasks

1 Decide what information each document should contain. Your teacher might be able to provide you with this information.
2 Produce each document using suitable software – a word-processor or a desktop publishing package. Each document should be well presented and make effective use of text-formatting methods.

■ *ICT Activity 2*

You see the following advertisement in a local newspaper.

WANTED

Sales assistant in a busy music and video store

Hours: 8.30 am–5.00 pm, five days each week

Duties: serving customers, taking care of new deliveries, keeping stock on the shelves in the right order.

We offer a competitive wage.

This vacancy would suit a school-leaver with good GCSEs or equivalent.

To apply please send a letter of application and a current CV to:

Freda Wind
Jumbo Records Ltd.
25 Broad Street
Lancton
LT2 5TY

You decide to apply for the position.

Task

Produce a letter of application and curriculum vitae (CV). Your CV should be written as though you have left school after obtaining your GCSE results.

HR functions: record keeping and training

Maintaining staff records

Businesses need to store data about their employees. The most important data is to do with the person's wages. This data is also used to calculate the taxes that the firm needs to pay the government.

The way these calculations are performed is covered in Unit 14. In this unit, we look at how the data is stored.

Most businesses store personnel data in a relational database (Unit 3). Personnel data is broken down into separate groups. Basic data such as name and address are stored in a separate file. Data about payments is stored in a payroll file. Data on how much tax the employer needs to pay to the government is stored in a taxation file. The business may also have a disciplinary file, which records action taken against members of staff who have broken the firm's rules.

The database needs a key field, which links all the database files together. The key field is usually something like a payroll number. This is a number unique to each employee. It can be used to identify a specific employee in the database. Each file will contain the key field.

In order to keep the data secure and confidential, the computer system will assign access rights to different users. For example, the accounts department may be able to see the data in the wages and taxation files but not the disciplinary files. Only the human resources (personnel) department may be able to see all the files. An individual employee may have the right to be shown what data the firm holds about them. But the employee may not have access to the database itself.

Training

The human resources department is usually responsible for meeting the employee's training needs.

One common way to identify training needs is for a manager to monitor the performance of the employee. The manager can then decide what training could be given to enable the employee to improve performance.

There are a number of different types of training.

Induction

Induction is the period at the start of a person's employment when the employee is settling into the new workplace. The employee is made familiar with the firm's rules and regulations, and health and safety requirements, and is generally made to feel at home.

Development

Development training enables employees to develop the skills and qualities they need in order to perform their job better and prepare for promotion.

In-house training

This is the name for any training that is carried out within the firm itself, either by its own employees or by trainers who are contracted in from another company (often the case with training for updated computer software, for example). The benefit of in-house training is that it is directly relevant to the jobs done by the firm's workers. A disadvantage is that if the firm has to employ specialist trainers, this can be relatively expensive, especially for a small firm.

In-house training means employees learn skills in the exact context where they will need to use them

External training

This is the name for all training that takes place outside the firm. It is usually done by large training organisations. An example would be a one-day course in using a particular type of software such as spreadsheets. A benefit for the employer is that it usually works out cheaper than if the firm organises the training itself. A problem is that the training may not be directly relevant to the specific needs of an individual business, as it will be designed as a service for any businesses within a particular industry (for example, publishers, caterers).

On-the-job training

On-the-job training occurs at the point where the job takes place. For example, a supermarket may ask an existing cashier to sit with a new employee and watch them operate a checkout till. A benefit of on-the-job training is that the employee receives directly relevant experience. Productive work can also take place at the same time. A problem is that the quality of the training may be poor. Also the employee may pick up bad working habits from the existing worker.

Off-the-job training

This takes place inside the firm but away from the main place of work. It is a type of internal training. For example, a cashier may be trained to operate a supermarket till that has been set up in a training room. A benefit is that the firm can organise the training so it is relevant to the needs of the job. A problem is that a training room is not as realistic a location as the actual place of work.

Training materials

Most firms will use publishing software to produce their own training materials. Firms can also purchase commercial training materials. These can include videos, books and computer software such as CD-ROMs and computer-based assessment materials. In computer-based assessment, the trainee is asked to perform a number of tasks using a computer. These may be multiple-choice questions or simple activities that can be used to assess the trainee and then direct them to a **learning strategy**.

■ *ICT Activity*

You work in the human resources department of a local supermarket. You have been asked to create an employee database. The database will store details of the supermarket's employees.

You are given the following information about each employee.

Name	Address	Telephone number	Date of birth	Position	Income last year	Number of days absent this year
Haroun Abib	23 The Limes, Duncton, DC5 6YY	01444-7345	24th Mar 1980	Cashier	£9,500	2
Ivor Morgan	5 Railway Lane, Duncton, DC2 6HV	01444-3498	30th Sep 1976	Driver	£16,000	1
Doug Witherfork	123B Biggles Road, Duncton, DC12 7HY	01444-4100	6th Feb 1967	Manager	£25,000	3
Madge Allbright	3 Closet Close, Binham, DC20 7BB	01444-6745	23rd Oct 1960	Cashier	£8,400	0
Kylie Donovan	45 Uplands Way, Duncton, DC10 5TR	01444-5316	9th Jul 1983	Cashier	£9,700	4
Eric Jackson	23 The Larches, Binham, DC20 7SA	01444-5643	17th Dec 1984	Deliveries assistant	£8,300	2
Phil Blandley	23 Staggs Drive, Duncton, DC4 5LP	01444-6846	23rd Apr 1981	Cashier	£8,900	2
Freda Payne	47 Gimley Crescent, Duncton, DC8 6CC	01444-9865	12th Mar 1976	Customer service	£12,600	1
Karen Goodyear	53 Old Hall Road, Binham, DC5 3DE	01444-8976	22nd Aug 1970	Assistant Manager	£18,000	0
Matilda Waltzer	120 Short Street, Duncton, DC10 4GG	01444-3456	30th May 1983	Customer service	£11,500	3

Tasks

1 Create the database.

- You need to decide what field names to give each kind of data.
- Your database program might also ask you what type of data is to be entered in each field. For example, the person's date of birth is a 'date-field', the address is a 'text-field' and the salary is a 'numerical-field'.
- Your database should contain a key field. You will need to decide what this should be.

2 Sort the database in order of income. The person with the highest income should appear first, the person with the lowest income should appear last.

3 Print a copy of your completed database.

4 Your manager has asked you to produce a report that displays all staff whose income last year was £10,000 or less. You are only required to display their name, position and income in the report.

5 Madge Allbright leaves the supermarket. Delete her from your database.

6 Dennis Midgely replaces Madge Allbright. His details are as follows: 24B Times Square, Duncton, DC3 3EE, 01444-9800, 24th Mar 1960, £8,500, 0. Add Dennis to your database.

7 Your manager asks you to add some more information to the database. The supermarket has asked all staff whether they are allergic to wheat or dairy products. The only members of staff who are allergic are Haroun (wheat) and Phil (dairy). Add this information to your database.

Businesses employ people. Unlike computers or other machines, which usually work constantly at the same rate, a person's productivity will be influenced by a number of different factors.

Motivation means the influences that cause a worker to operate at a particular level of efficiency. People who are highly motivated will generally work harder and more effectively than people who lack motivation.

In order to motivate a worker, the business needs to know what that person wants to gain from the job. The firm will then be able to provide the person with incentives. These should then motivate the worker to perform to the best of his or her ability.

Reasons why people work

People choose to work for a number of different reasons. Some of the most common reasons are outlined below.

To satisfy basic needs

Our basic human needs are to have enough food, clothing, warmth and shelter in order to stay alive. For most people in the UK, these needs are met by receiving a wage or salary that can buy what is required.

As well as these physical needs, some people argue that we have basic social needs that can also be met through work. These include meeting other people, having a sense of belonging to a larger group, and the status that comes from having a well-regarded job.

To earn an income

Once we have earned an income to cover our basic physical needs, we can then use the money left over to buy luxuries that can increase our standard of living. These include any items that go beyond what we *need* for our physical survival – for example, cars, dishwashers and holidays.

The chance to buy a desirable object such as a car can be highly motivational for some people

To gain job satisfaction

Some people gain satisfaction from doing a good job. They like to be rewarded with praise and recognition.

To develop a career

Some people are motivated by ambition, or the will to succeed. They want to do well in their job so that they can be promoted into more senior and powerful jobs.

Motivation methods

In order to increase employees' motivation, the firm must put in place systems that tap into the reasons why people work. Such systems include the following.

Payment systems

These are covered in Unit 14.

Improving communication systems

People like to feel that their employer values them. They like to feel that the business believes that their opinion is important.

Communicating with employees is a way of making sure that they feel valued. The firm could make sure that its staff is kept informed of the latest developments within the business. It could hold meetings, or use a bulletin board. ICT developments mean that the firm can use e-mail or an intranet to communicate with staff. The firm could also make sure that it consults staff – it could ask them for their opinions about the way that the firm is run. ICT can make this process easier to manage.

Job rotation

Job rotation aims to prevent the boredom that comes from doing the same job all day and every day.

The firm may ask its staff to change jobs, perhaps every two weeks. A good example of job rotation might be in a supermarket, where a person is asked to work on the cheese counter one day and on a checkout desk the next.

A benefit of job rotation is that it keeps workers from being bored. Unfortunately, it can mean that one repetitive job is simply replaced with another.

Job enlargement

When someone starts a new job, their **productivity level** is often low. This is because they do not yet know the most efficient way to perform the job. When they have been doing the job for a while they become more efficient. This means they can do the same amount of work in less time. **Job enlargement** is when the business fills this spare time with more tasks for the person to perform.

A benefit is that productive workers are able to produce more work. Unfortunately, some people might think that their efficiency is being 'punished'!

Job enrichment

This is very similar to job enlargement. The only difference is that instead of doing more of the same work, the employee is asked to do supervisory or managerial work. For example, an operative could be given **job enrichment** by being asked to provide on-the-job training to new members of staff.

Teamworking

Most people do not do their job on their own – they work with other people. Sometimes they will all be doing the same job – for example, a group of people who all stitch collars onto shirts in a clothing factory. Sometimes people will each be contributing to a different stage of the same job – for example, a group of workers where each makes a different part of the same shirt.

Teamworking organises people into groups who work towards the same objectives. This helps to create a team spirit and so meets some social needs of the workers. The team can also be asked to take responsibility for its own work. The team can supervise itself. Some people think that this can make the team members more motivated.

■ *ICT Activity*

Mateson Jordan PLC is a company that makes and sells a range of kitchen and bathroom equipment. The firm has over 5000 employees in ten different locations throughout the UK.

You have been asked to create a newsletter that can keep the employees up to date with the latest developments in the company.

You have been provided with the following list of recent news items.

- Mateson Jordan has recently won a contract to supply all the schools in Lancashire with new toilet seats. This will safeguard jobs in the Duncton factory for the next six months. Sales manager Sheila Peer says this is excellent news for everyone in the company.
- Doris Whitely last month completed forty years continuous service in the accounts department. Company managing director Arthur Jordan presented her with a silver clock.
- Duncton telephone sales assistant Serena Page last month completed a cycle ride from Lands End to John O'Groats. She raised over £10,000 for charity.
- The Duncton factory football team reached the quarter finals of the Duncton and District Football Cup. They beat Farrow Rovers 4–3. Gary Duckett, a porcelain-finisher, scored the winning goal.

Task

Use the above information to create a one-page newsletter. You can add more detail to the stories or add additional stories. You should use either a word-processor or desktop publishing software. The newsletter should be as professional-looking as possible. Use appropriate graphics or photographs to illustrate the stories.

Payment systems

In this unit, we look at how businesses pay their employees. Businesses have to pay competitive rates to their employees. Firms who do not pay their workers enough might find that staff leave to work elsewhere. They may also find it difficult to recruit new staff. A business must decide on the type of payment system to use. Each payment method will have a different impact on the way that employees are motivated. This is because each method links pay to the worker's performance in different ways.

Payment methods

Salaries

A **salary** is a fixed amount of money paid to an employee. Salaries are usually paid monthly. For example, a person whose salary is £12,000 a year will be paid £1,000 each month. The amount received is therefore unrelated to the day-to-day work performance of the individual.

A benefit of a salary is that both the employer and employee know exactly how much income the person will receive. This can help the firm calculate its costs. A problem is that a salary does not link pay to performance in any way. The employee's income will stay the same even if they work longer hours.

Wages: time rates

A **wage** is the name given to a payment in return for a specific amount of work. Wages are usually calculated as a fixed amount per hour worked. For example, a person earning £5 per hour who works 40 hours per week will earn a wage of £200.

A problem with **time rate** wages is that employees may try to work for as many hours as possible, because the longer they work the more they earn. This means that the work must be supervised to make sure that it is completed on time.

Wages: piece rates

With **piece rates,** the unit used to calculate the wage is a specific task. For example, a worker stitching collars in a shirt factory may be paid a piece rate of 20 pence for each collar stitched. So if the person stitches 20 collars in an hour they would earn £4.

A benefit of piece rate wages is that they give an incentive to the worker to work as quickly as possible. This should improve their work rate and so boost productivity. A big problem is that producing the work quickly may mean that quality suffers. The work needs to be supervised to make sure that it is of an acceptable standard.

Bonuses and commission

Bonuses are one-off payments that reward performance meeting a particular target. For example, a workforce that produces more than the target number of televisions might receive a bonus of £200 for each worker.

Commission is usually paid to sales staff and is related to the value or number of orders that they take. This incentive is designed to encourage the sales staff to win as many orders as possible.

Gross pay and net pay

A person employed on an annual salary of £35,000 will not receive **take-home pay** of £35,000. In order to pay income tax and national insurance, the employer will deduct, or take away, approximately £8,000 of the salary.

Gross pay is the name given to the total amount of the salary or wage before any deductions. **Net pay** is what the employee is free to spend after income tax and national insurance have been deducted.

Take-home pay is net pay – what is left after deductions

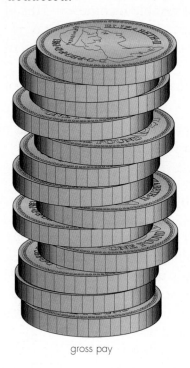

gross pay

net pay

You need to know how both income tax and national insurance are calculated.

Income tax

Income tax is the main tax collected by the government. It is taken from everyone who earns an income from any source. The most common way is through employment, but income tax is also collected from the interest earned on bank savings.

The most common method of paying income tax is called Pay As You Earn (PAYE). With this method the employer deducts the income tax from the employee's pay before they ever see it. The main benefit to employees is that they do not have to worry about paying one large tax bill at the end of the year.

Tax-free allowance is part of a person's earnings on which no income tax has to be paid (the first £4,385 of the salary, in 2000 to 2001 – see below). This is so that people on very low incomes (below £4,385) do not pay any income tax. **Taxable income** is all the income above this level, which the government can tax.

The following figures explain how the income tax of a person aged between 18 and 65 was calculated during the tax year 2000 to 2001. (Up-to-date figures are available on the internet at www.inlandrevenue.gov.uk.)

Tax-free allowance of £4,385	no tax paid on earnings below £4,385
First £1,520 of taxable income	10% of this income paid in tax
Next £26,880 of taxable income	22% of this income paid in tax
All remaining taxable income	40% of this income paid in tax

What happens to the amount of tax paid as people's incomes increase? Why do you think this is so?

Example

In the tax year 2000 to 2001, a person earned £35,000.

The first £4,385 of earnings was tax free. No income tax was paid on this income. The next slice of income was £1,520 – 10% tax was paid, which equalled £152. The next slice of income was £26,880, of which 22% was paid in tax, equal to £5,914.

The three slices so far add up to £32,785 (£4,385 + £1,520 + £26,880). This means that the person's taxable income in the 40% taxable income band was £35,000 – £32,785 = £2215. The person paid 40% of this, which was £886.

So the total income tax paid was £152 + £5,914 + £886 = £6952.

Note that income tax is calculated using total earnings for the whole year.

National insurance

The government uses national insurance contributions to fund the money given to people who are temporarily unemployed. It is also used to pay the **state pension** to people who have retired from work.

National insurance is much simpler to calculate than income tax. It is based on the weekly income.

In the tax year 2000 to 2001, national insurance was deducted at the rate of 10% of all gross weekly income between £76 and £535.

Example

A person earning £35,000 a year receives an average weekly income of £673. In 2000 to 2001, the person paid national insurance of £45.90 each week – that is, 10% of the difference between £535 and £76.

Anyone earning less than £76 per week will not pay any national insurance. Anyone earning over £535 will pay the same national insurance of £45.90, regardless of the size of their income.

■ *ICT Case study*

Sally Jessup works as a sales manager in a busy travel agency. Her gross salary is £30,000 a year. She is offered a promotion to become an area sales manager for a number of travel agents. This will mean more responsibility and working an extra five hours a week. Her new salary will be £36,000 a year.

Tasks

1 Calculate Sally's net income after she has paid income tax and national insurance. Work this out both for her current income and for what she will earn if she accepts the promotion. Use the rates that applied in 2000 to 2001.
2 How much will her annual net pay go up if she accepts the promotion?
3 How much extra per week is this?
4 Do you think that Sally should accept the promotion? Explain your answer.

■ *ICT Activity*

Workers at Broome's Supermarket are paid an hourly wage. The current hourly wage is £4.20/hour for cashiers and £4.80/hour for customer service assistants.

The following is a list of hours worked in the past week for a number of staff:

Name	Hours worked
Cashiers:	
Brian	37
Shirley	35
Claire	24
Sally	20
Chris	36
Bob	40
Customer service assistants:	
Maria	36
Bethan	27
Mike	34

Tasks

1 Create a spreadsheet that can be used to calculate automatically the weekly wage payable to each worker. Add a formula to calculate the average weekly wage.

2 The following week everyone works the same hours, but the company decides to give all workers a 10% wage increase. Change the formulas and re-calculate the average weekly wage.

Businesses employ people, and all the people in the organisation need to know what they should be doing. Effective **communication** methods are required to make sure that information is given and received correctly.

There are a number of different methods that can be used to communicate information from one part of the business to another. Each method has its advantages and disadvantages. It is important that the right medium is used to carry the message. It is also important that the right technology is used to transmit the information. In this unit, we look at the main methods of communication. We also see how the use of ICT is increasing the speed of communication.

Main communication methods

Verbal communication

Verbal communication is the most commonly used method. It takes place when one person explains something to others.

Humans will always use verbal communication

A benefit of verbal communication is that it is quick and easy to use. Speakers can use the tone of their voice and particular language to indicate their mood. It is also possible to get instant feedback from listeners, which can be used to check that they have understood the message. Unfortunately, there is no permanent record of the communication – it is possible to forget something that you have been told.

Some examples of verbal communication methods in business are described below.

Telephone

The telephone can be used to speak with people in a different location. A specific limitation of telephone conversations is that the callers can't see one another. This means that body language and gestures can't be seen. The voice is the only medium that can be used to carry the message. However, telephones that are able to capture and transmit digital images are now being used by the media and in business. For example, small portable devices combining a video camera and a satellite transmitter are being used by television journalists to transmit moving images from remote areas. This technology is still being developed, to improve the image resolution and reduce the cost.

Telephone communication has been vital in business for many years

Mobile telephones

The main benefit of mobile phones to businesses is that they can be used to keep in contact with employees who are out of the office.

Voice-mail

Voice-mail is linked to the telephone and allows people to leave messages. The recipient can listen and respond to them later. Voice-mail stores the telephone message digitally. This means that memory space is limited on some systems. However, it has the advantage that the recipient can select which messages to keep and which ones to delete.

Discussions

These are informal conversations between two or more people, of which no permanent record is normally made, though important decisions can be reached. Traditionally such meetings have had to be made face to face, but the introduction of video-conferencing (Unit 4) has meant that informal discussions can take place between people in different offices. This technology also has the advantage that the discussions can be recorded if a permanent record is needed.

Meetings

These are formal conversations between two or more people. A meeting usually has an **agenda**, which is a list of the topics that will be discussed. After the meeting, a permanent record of what was discussed is produced. This is called the **minutes** of the meeting. Agendas and minutes are usually produced using a word-processor. The basic layout of the agenda and minutes can be stored on a template, which can then be opened and adapted for the particular meeting. These documents can be e-mailed to the participants in the meeting. E-mail helps to speed up the communication process and can reduce the amount of paper needed.

Business meetings follow a more formal structure than discussions

Presentations

When a person speaks to a group of people about an issue or idea, he or she is making a **presentation**. The speaker often complements the speech with a slide show. This can be used to emphasise the main points of the presentation.

A benefit of a presentation is that important information can be communicated to a large group of people. A drawback of this form of communication is that the audience mainly listens to the speaker – there is little opportunity for dialogue between the speaker and the audience. Speakers are increasingly using presentation software to prepare materials to use in presentations (Unit 5).

Written communication

Writing is a very important business communication method. The main benefit is that a permanent record can be kept of the communication. Written methods are also useful for communicating complex information. A problem with written communication is that it is slower than verbal methods. Also, the person reading it may misunderstand the message if it is badly worded or ambiguous.

Examples of written communications used in business include the following. Any or all of these can be transmitted as printed documents or electronic ones.

- Letters communicate information to people outside the business. They are used when a permanent record is required. An example might be a reply to a sales enquiry.
- Memorandums (memos) communicate information to people inside the organisation. An example might be a request for a new computer system.
- Messages give specific information to people in the business when no permanent record is needed. An example is a message to ask a salesperson to telephone a customer.
- Notices communicate information to large numbers of people. An example might be a notice informing staff of the date for a Christmas party.
- Reports are lengthy documents that analyse an issue in detail. Reports provide managers and directors with the information they need in order to take important decisions. An example might be a report comparing the performance of two rival computer systems.
- Minutes provide a permanent record of the discussions held at a meeting. They are given to all the participants after the meeting.

■ Newsletters communicate general information to all the employees of the company. They are an important way of helping to create a sense of community. This is particularly important if the business employs lots of people.

Electronic communication methods

Modern technology has given us a number of new pieces of equipment and methods of communicating. Three of them – e-mail, video-conferencing and facsimiles (fax) – were covered in Unit 4. Here we look at some more.

Text-messaging

Mobile telephone technology can be used to transmit and receive simple **text-messages**. Text-messages can be used rather like e-mail to send information to a large number of staff. Most mobile phone systems limit the number of characters that can be transmitted in a single message and so users have to abbreviate (shorten) words and phrases in order to make the message fit within the character limit. Next-generation mobile phones will enable more complex data to be transmitted, including internet pages and moving images. Pagers can *receive* text-messages. They cannot be used to *send* messages.

Portable computers including hand-held devices

Portable computers work like normal desktop personal computers. The main differences are that they are smaller, lighter and battery-powered, though most portable computers can run on mains electricity, too. They can also be connected to other computers in order to transfer data from one to the other.

As computers become more powerful, hand-held computers are becoming more popular. They are sometimes called palm-top computers. These look like miniature computers. They contain simple word-processing, spreadsheet and database software. Some can also connect to the internet.

The main benefit of portable computers to a business is that the employee can carry out productive work even when travelling from one office to another.

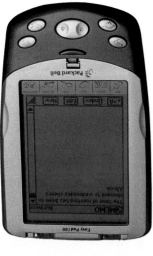

Even the tiniest palm-top computer can contain a lot of processing power

Improving communication

Communication is the act of transmitting and receiving information. It is therefore a two-way process. It is not enough to assume that because a message has been given, it must have been received and understood.

Many mistakes in history have been the results of poor communication. For example, the infamous 'Charge of the Light Brigade' happened because one military commander failed to understand the message given to him by his commanding officer. The problem was that the message given was ambiguous. This is the most common reason for miscommunication.

Consequences of poor communication for a business can include:

■ poor morale inside the company if employees feel they are not being listened to
■ poor customer relations if the firm misunderstands an order from a customer.

The benefits of good communication can include:

■ good employee relations, especially if workers feel valued by the firm
■ good customer relations and repeat orders from happy customers.

Throughout this unit, we have looked at different methods of communication, including ICT. There are two main ways that increased use of ICT can improve communications for a business.

1 ICT can cut down the time it takes to transmit information. E-mail and mobile phones can put people in touch very quickly. This means there can be more time to check that the information was received and understood properly. This will help to reduce the number of communication errors.

2 ICT can enable the same message to be given to large numbers of people at once – for example, using e-mail or text-messaging. A presentation can be prepared and made available for people to download and view from the internet. This enables more people to be involved and so increases their sense of belonging to the organisation. This can help to increase their motivation (Unit 13).

■ ICT Activity

You work in the customer service department of Samson Motors, a large second-hand car dealer. The address is 23–36 Milton Drive, Freshley, FS3 3FG.

You receive the following memorandum from the Sales Manager.

MEMORANDUM

To: *Customer service department*

From: *Diana Knightly, Sales Manager*

Date: *1st April 2003*

Subject: *Customer complaint*

We received a telephone complaint today from a Mr Drawl, 23 The Limes, Freshley, FS3 3TT.

He said that the new Ford Escort he bought yesterday has a faulty radio. He says that the cassette player does not work.

Please send him a letter asking him to bring the car along to our garage. One of our mechanics will look at it. If he can't fix it there and then we will order a replacement. These usually take about two/three weeks to arrive. Please tell him that this kind of thing hasn't happened before and that we are very sorry for the inconvenience.

P.S. Don't make any spelling mistakes, like you did last time!

Task

Write the letter. When you have finished the letter, send the sales manager a memorandum telling her that you have done what she asked.

Work through these questions to check your knowledge of each unit.

■ 10 HR functions: job roles and working conditions

1 Identify two functions that the directors of a business carry out.

2 Explain the difference between a manager and a supervisor.

3 What is the difference between a supervisor and an operative?

4 a) What is teleworking?
   b) Give two benefits and two drawbacks of teleworking for an employee.

5 a) What is hotdesking?
   b) Give two benefits of hotdesking to an employer.

■ 11 HR functions: recruitment

1 Jafferson Kielder, a large insurance firm, is thinking of recruiting a new insurance sales person. Draw a diagram to illustrate the seven main stages of the recruitment process.

2 Explain two ways that job analysis can be carried out.

3 What is the difference between a job description and a person specification?

4 Jafferson Kielder is unsure where to find the right person for the job. Identify and explain four different methods they could use to make people aware of the vacancy.

5 Some firms will ask to see a copy of each candidate's CV. What is a CV?

6 Write out four questions that Jafferson Kielder could ask each candidate in an interview.

7 How can ICT help make the recruitment process easier to manage?

■ 12 HR functions: record keeping and training

1 Why do firms need to store information about their employees?

2 Which law covers the use of computer data by a business?

3 A firm stores employee names and addresses in a 'employee' data file and information about pay in a 'payroll' file. What type of database does the firm use?

4 A firm stores confidential information about each employee on its computer system. How could the business ensure that only authorised people are able to access this information?

5 A supermarket makes sure that all new employees are told about the organisation's health and safety policy on their first day at work. What type of training is being given?

6 The supermarket expects new cashiers to learn how to do the job by watching experienced cashiers work.
   a) What type of training is this?
   b) Give one benefit and one drawback of this type of training, to the supermarket.

7 The supermarket arranges for a trainee store manager to attend a Business Studies course at the local college every Thursday afternoon.
   a) What type of training is this?
   b) Give one benefit and one drawback of this type of training, to the supermarket.

8 Explain how ICT can be used to improve the quality of in-house training.

■ 13 Motivation

1 **a)** Identify three different reasons why people might wish to work for an employer.
   b) For each reason you identified in **(a)** explain what an employer could do to motivate the worker.

2 Explain the difference between job rotation and job enlargement. For each one, say why it might help to motivate a worker and say why it might have the opposite effect.

3 What does job enrichment mean? How might it help to motivate an employee?

4 What is meant by teamworking? Examine the arguments for and against teamworking.

■ 14 Payment systems

1 Why is it important for firms to pay their staff a competitive wage or salary?

2 Explain the difference between a wage and a salary.

3 Explain how piece rate wages are calculated. How are the incentive effects of piece rate wages different to those of time rate wages?

4 Sales staff at a mobile phone retailer are paid £25 each time a customer buys a new mobile phone package. What is this payment method called? What incentives will this payment method give to the sales staff?

5 What two things are deducted from an employee's gross income before they receive their net income?

6 Why do most employees prefer to pay their tax using the PAYE method?

7 In 2000 to 2001, the top rate of income tax was 40%. This was paid on all income above £32,785. What was different about the top rate of national insurance contributions?

8 Use a spreadsheet software package to develop a spreadsheet that contains the appropriate formulas to calculate the tax and national insurance to be paid by employees on PAYE.

9 Use the information from Unit 14 to calculate the following.
   a) How much tax will an employee pay on the PAYE system if he earns £24,000 per annum?
   b) How much tax will an employee pay on the PAYE system if she earns £48,000 per annum?
   c) Explain the difference between the two tax bills you have calculated in (b).
   d) How much national insurance will these two employees have to pay?

■ 15 Communication systems

1 Identify and explain four different methods of verbal communication.

2 Identify and explain four different methods of written communication.

3 How is a memorandum different from a letter?

4 John in the Bristol office has a message that he urgently needs to give to Peter in the London office. The message is fairly complex but there is no need to keep a permanent copy. Explain which communication method you would recommend John uses.

5 Jane, the sales manager, has a message that she would like all members of her sales team to receive. The message is quite long and Jane would like each sales person to keep a permanent copy of the message. Each member of the team only visits the office about once a month, but they all have a mobile phone and a laptop computer.
   a) Identify two appropriate communication methods that Jane could use.
   b) List the pros and cons of each method and say which method you recommend Jane should use.

6 Explain two problems that could result in a business as a result of poor communication between the sales department and the production department.

7 Explain two ways in which ICT can help to improve the flow of communication around a business.

Section 4

Workplace organisation and production

16

Workplace organisation: location and the working environment

Location

Traditionally, when choosing a location, most businesses have had to decide between two options.

1 They could locate near to the main source of raw materials, in order to cut down the cost of transporting them. For example, the steel industry needs coal for energy and iron to make the steel. Both of these are bulky and heavy and so very expensive to transport. Both are used during the production process. So traditionally steel producers located production close to coal-fields and supplies of iron ore.

2 They could locate near to the main customers, or employment opportunities, in order to cut down the cost of transporting the finished product, or recruiting a labour force. An example of an industry that has chosen this type of location historically is glass manufacture. The raw materials are relatively easy to transport, and so the factory can be located near to urban areas. Due to the nature of the finished product, breakages can be minimised by having the raw materials transported to the factory and glassware having to be transported a shorter distance. Being in an urban location also means that there will be employment opportunities for the local people, without them having to travel great distances to find work.

Manufacturing Waterford glass. Glass manufacturers are traditionally located near to their customers

Hi-tech industries such as electronics can be located anywhere, because transport costs of both their raw materials and their products are low

Most modern businesses do not face these location issues. In particular, **e-commerce** firms can locate anywhere in the world where they can recruit people with the relevant skills. E-commerce businesses make their products available via the internet. This means that the customer can purchase from anywhere in the world – all they require is access to the internet.

Most firms in the service sector can also locate pretty much anywhere. If you telephone an insurance company, for example, you will probably speak to a person in a call centre. A **call centre** is a large office that handles a firm's telephone enquiries. The operators will take customer orders and answer account queries. The call centre can be located anywhere that has enough telephone capacity and a large supply of potential employees.

Office design

The layout of call centre and e-commerce offices very much depends on the type of work that is done there. But all modern offices generally share the same basic design features.

Layout

Modern offices are either open-plan or cellular.

- **Open-plan offices** have no dividing walls between the different workstations on each floor. Everyone in the office can see the work of everyone else. The basic idea is to improve communications by enabling staff to move around the office quickly. Open-plan offices are also more flexible. Different operations can be expanded or contracted without having to move dividing walls.
- **Cellular offices** divide the floor area into separate, smaller offices. Senior managers who need to hold discussions in private often use these offices.

In practice, most offices use a combination of the two layouts. For example, there might be an open-plan area in the middle of the office for the main operatives and supervisors. Around the outside, there could be cellular offices for senior managers.

The key issue for a business in designing its office area is to consider whether the work carried out by a person needs to be kept confidential. If it doesn't, they are likely to be given space in an open-plan area.

Accommodating ICT

Modern offices are also built to accommodate the infrastructure needed to run large computer systems. For example, the cables needed to carry data across the firm's computer network are hidden above ceilings or below floors. Individual workstations can be linked up by plugging a connecting cable into a network data socket. This can help reduce some of the health and safety risks associated with trailing computer leads (Unit 9).

The easy networking of computer terminals (Unit 17) has contributed to the increased use of hotdesking. Each work-desk has a computer attached to the network that any worker can use to access the files they need. Information on the network can also be accessed remotely via telephone lines, which has resulted in teleworking – some workers no longer need to be at the office at all, but can produce their work at home (Unit 10).

Taking the concept of teleworking a step further means that some staff no longer need to be employed by the firm full-time. Some companies have introduced a division between 'core workers' and 'peripheral workers'. Core workers are employed full-time by the firm and usually work at the company's offices. Peripheral workers contribute on a part-time or temporary basis and usually work from home.

Ergonomics

Ergonomics is the study of the way that workers react to their working environment. 'Sick-building syndrome' is a well-known phenomenon meaning that badly designed working environments can result in workers taking more time off sick. Sometimes this can be the result of specific problems, such as poorly ventilated air-conditioning systems. But more commonly it is the result of things like a lack of sufficient daylight. A worker in the middle of an open-plan office may be a long way from the nearest window and so not get any daylight.

ICT can help. Computer-aided design software (CAD) can be used to design buildings in such a way that the impact of poor office design on workers is identified and assessed. The firm can then model different designs and predict the impact these designs will have upon the staff. They can identify both the cost of the building and the benefit of reduced sickness. Some of the safety issues resulting from excessive use of computer equipment were covered in Unit 9.

■ *ICT Activity*

You work as a journalist for the *Freshley Gazette*, the biggest-selling quality local newspaper in the Freshley area.

You have been asked to prepare an article for the newspaper on the effects of new working methods such as hotdesking and teleworking.

Tasks

1 As part of your research, design a short questionnaire. Use it to obtain information from friends and family about how they have been affected by recent changes in working methods.

2 If possible, carry out some research on the internet. For example, you could look at other newspaper articles that have been written on this subject.

3 When you have completed your research, write the article using publishing software.

17

Workplace organisation: storing and sharing information

Businesses store large amounts of data on their computer systems. Some of this data needs to be kept confidential because of the Data Protection Act (Unit 9). Some of the data would be very useful if it got into the hands of the firm's competitors. All of the data would be at risk if viruses got into the computer system.

For these reasons, all businesses need to take steps to make sure that their computer systems and the data contained on them are kept secure.

Security threats

Hackers can use ICT to access all kinds of restricted data, including people's bank accounts and PIN details

The two main threats to data security are hackers and viruses. **Hackers** are people who gain unauthorised access to computer systems or files. A hacker could be a member of staff who gains access to a restricted part of the network. A computer **virus** is a program that corrupts or damages other computer files (Unit 4).

WELCOME
TO THE
BANK

The risks are increased if data is stored on a **computer network**. Computer networks consist of a number of workstations that are connected to the network **file-server**. This is the central computer that stores the files used on the network.

There are two main types of network

1 Local area networks (**LAN**s) are connected together using cable, or more recently, wireless signals. The workstations are permanently connected to each other. Any workstation on the network could, in theory, access all the data stored on the network. Most schools network their computers together using a LAN.
2 Wide area networks (**WAN**s) are temporary connections between computers. The data is transmitted using the telephone network. They are often used to connect together computers in different offices. For example, a computer in a branch office could use a WAN to connect to the head office network. This means that it is possible for a hacker to gain access to the network from any computer in the world. The internet is an example of a WAN.

A particular problem in recent years has been the theft of laptop computers from people on trains. Sometimes thieves are more interested in accessing the data from it than in obtaining the computer itself.

Protecting computer systems

There are a number of different ways that businesses can protect their computer systems.

Preventing physical access to computer systems

One way to prevent access to computer files is to prevent people from using the computers in the first place! The easiest way to do this is to keep computer rooms locked when they are not being used. It is also possible to put locks on keyboards. To help recover goods if stolen, computers and all other equipment should have the owner's name marked onto them, ideally using ink that is invisible to the thief, but visible under ultra-violet light.

Preventing access to data on the network

Usernames and passwords

The most common way to prevent access to files on a network is to set up the system so that **usernames** and **passwords** are required. These should be sequences of characters that the user can remember, but that are not obvious to anyone else. Things like the names of favourite football teams should be avoided as passwords because they are easy to guess. Passwords should never be written down. They should also be frequently changed.

Access levels

Access levels can be assigned to different types of information. For example, the directors of a company will be given access to more information than operatives in the sales department. Only the network managers will have access to the files that control the network.

Firewalls

Firewalls can be installed. These help to keep the various parts of the network separate from each other. They might prevent a virus infecting the whole network. Someone who has managed to hack into one part of a network would be unable to gain access to other parts.

Data encryption

Hackers can intercept data sent across the telephone network. This is a particular problem when using a wide area network such as the internet – for example, when sending credit card details to shop on-line. **Encryption** software can keep the data secure by turning it into a scrambled code. The receiving computer can only decode the data if it has the same encryption software and it knows the correct encryption code. In practice, this makes it very unlikely that a hacker could read the data.

Back-up files

Hackers and viruses can damage computer data. It is therefore vital that firms keep back-up copies of all important files. Backing-up files usually takes place at night, or some other quiet time. It is important to keep the back-up files secure. It would be sensible to store them in a different location to the place where the file-server is kept.

Use of emergency procedures

It is sensible for network managers to have contingency plans that they can carry out if there is a threat to the security of the computer system. These plans could include:

- backing-up system files and data if there is a risk of fire or flood damage – as a last resort, the network could be closed down
- instructing all staff not to use e-mail if there is a risk of a virus – as a last resort, the wide area network could be disconnected and connections to the internet removed
- instructing all staff to change their password if one is accidentally revealed to an unauthorised person
- removing access rights to an individual if he or she is believed to be breaking the firm's security rules.

■ *ICT Activity*

You are employed as the computer network manager for a telephone banking business. Customers telephone the bank's call centre and an operative then accesses the person's account and processes their requests.

You have been asked to write a memorandum to all telephone operatives. The memorandum should explain how the bank ensures that customer information is kept confidential.

Task

Produce the memorandum using word-processing software. You should use the information in this unit. You can also use any other relevant information.

File management

Most people who work with computers quickly generate a large number of files. Without good file management it would be difficult to find a particular file. There are a number of features of good file management.

Saving files with names that indicate their content

Filenames are important. They are often the only way of locating the information stored on a computer. The filename should enable the user to know what the file contains. Most modern software allows you to create filenames over 200 characters long!
Different versions of files should be labelled with version numbers. For example, the first draft of a leaflet could be called Leaflet01, the second draft would then be called Leaflet02, and so on.

Organising related files into directories

Files are stored within a hierarchy of folders, designed to make it easy for you to find what you want

Another name for a **directory** is a **folder**. The name of the folder should also give an indication of its contents. Folders can be stored inside folders, so it is possible to organise the files using a **hierarchical system**. The user searches down through a series of folders until they find the file they are looking for.

File   Edit   View   Window   Special   Help

◻   Macintosh HD

52 items, 52.90 GB available

Name	Date Modified	Size	Kind
▷ 🗀 Applications	Wed, Oct 24, 2001, 9:04 pm	—	folder
▽ 🗀 Applications (Mac OS 9)	Wed, Oct 24, 2001, 3:24 pm	—	folder
▽ 🗀 Acrobat Reader 4.0	Fri, Aug 3, 2001, 12:22 am	—	folder
📄 Acrobat™ Reader 4.0	Tue, Nov 2, 1999, 9:00 pm	4.9 MB	application program
▽ 🗀 Help	Fri, Aug 3, 2001, 12:22 am	—	folder
▽ 🗀 ENU	Fri, Aug 3, 2001, 12:22 am	—	folder
📄 Acrobat.pdf	Thu, Oct 21, 1999, 7:38 pm	52 K	Acrobat Reader 5.0 document
📄 READER.PDF	Thu, Oct 21, 1999, 7:40 pm	408 K	Acrobat Reader 5.0 document
▽ 🗀 Plug-Ins	Fri, Aug 3, 2001, 12:22 am	—	folder
▽ 🗀 AcroForm	Fri, Aug 3, 2001, 12:22 am	—	folder
📄 AcroFill	Tue, Oct 26, 1999, 9:00 pm	884 K	Acrobat Reader 5.0 document
▷ 🗀 JavaScripts	Fri, Aug 3, 2001, 12:22 am	—	folder
▷ 🗀 EFS	Fri, Aug 3, 2001, 12:22 am	—	folder
▷ 🗀 EWH	Fri, Aug 3, 2001, 12:22 am	—	folder
▷ 🗀 HLS	Fri, Aug 3, 2001, 12:22 am	—	folder
▷ 🗀 Movie	Fri, Aug 3, 2001, 12:22 am	—	folder
▷ 🗀 WebBuy	Fri, Aug 3, 2001, 12:22 am	—	folder
▷ 🗀 WebLink	Fri, Aug 3, 2001, 12:22 am	—	folder

Saving open files at regular intervals

Once a file is saved it is stored permanently on the computer's backing storage. When you open a file and work on it, any changes to the file are first stored on the computer's internal **RAM** or temporary memory (RAM stands for random access memory). If the computer loses power or **crashes** while you have the file open, this RAM data is lost forever. For this reason, it is important to save at regular and frequent intervals as you work on a file.

Searching for files

It is possible to search for files that meet certain criteria or contain certain **keywords**. Some file management systems allow you to tag information about the file onto it. For example, you can write the name of the author and give a description of the file's contents. You can also specify the keywords that the file management system will look for.

■ *ICT Case study*

Gift e-retailers know about the crushing workload the Christmas season can bring. Last year, ICT staff at one major internet shop kept business executives, marketing staff and product line managers abreast of sales information by pulling together daily reports on sales for each member of the management.

'We do not want to go through that again,' said the director of data warehousing. 'Essentially, every report was a one-off. Instead, we need an environment where we can manage data access and security, and produce one report that will serve many purposes.'

This year, to manage data on a growing product list, the company aims to install new e-business intelligence software, just in time for the Christmas rush.

'That's when you're going to capture a lot of that critical customer data,' said the ICT manager. 'It's important for retailers to understand which customers are profitable and which aren't.'

The software consists of three main elements.

■ The 'Web Server' offers product and customer data – such as number of items sold, prices of items sold, order sources and customer profile information – which is formatted into database files.
■ An authoring tool, 'Web Reports', can then be used to arrange data from the files into formats that can be published on-line.
■ The third element, 'Query', is designed to allow users to personalise a report, picking the data items they want and choosing how those items will be filtered and sorted.

All company managers will have access to the same web interface, but none knows the specific data sources they're using. High-level executives will design user classes that decide the level of data to which each user has access. They may not, for example, wish to make product profit margin data and other financially sensitive information available to every user.

This system will cost over £100,000 to implement, but the company is convinced that it will pay for itself through improved data preparation, storage and retrieval, thereby making the company as a whole more efficient.

Tasks

1 Describe how the use of on-line support can help workers that carry out tasks away from the central office.
2 Describe two disadvantages of using an on-line support system for the workers in the field (away from the central office) and two disadvantages for the workers in the data centre (where the database is managed).
3 Produce a report on the use of centrally held data in the retail trade.

18 Production: costs and break-even analysis

The main objective of most businesses is to make profit. Profit is the difference between the income from selling products (**revenue**) and the cost of running the business. In this unit, we look at how the business can calculate its costs and revenues. We also look at a useful technique that tells the firm how many products it needs to sell in order to begin making a profit.

Calculating costs

A firm's costs are usually broken up into two main types.

- **Variable cost**, also known as direct cost, is the cost of making the firm's products. Elements of variable cost include things like the cost of raw materials, wages of production workers and the cost of operating production equipment. The value of variable cost will change if the level of output changes.
- **Fixed cost**, also known as indirect cost, is the cost of running the business as a whole. Elements of fixed cost include the salaries of head office workers and the cost of running advertising campaigns. Fixed cost will not change even if the level of production changes.

'Variable cost' added to 'fixed cost' gives the firm's 'total cost'. If the firm knows its total cost and the level of production, it can calculate its average cost, otherwise known as **unit cost** (that is, the total cost of producing each individual product item).

$$\text{variable cost} + \text{fixed cost} = \text{total cost}$$

$$\frac{\text{total cost}}{\text{output}} = \text{average cost, or unit cost}$$

Break-even analysis

Break-even analysis can be used to find out the minimum level of output needed to fully cover the firm's costs. Any output above the break-even point will result in the firm making a profit. In order to calculate the break-even level of output, the firm needs to know:

- the total fixed cost
- the variable cost per unit of output
- the selling price.

Variable cost per unit of output is equal to the variable cost of making each individual product item. The easiest way to calculate it, is to divide the total variable cost by the level of output (that is, the number of product items made).

The table gives the cost and revenue data for an imaginary firm. As you can see, the firm's break-even level of output is at 500 units. This data can be illustrated using a break-even chart, as shown below.

The total revenue matches the total cost at the break-even point – the profit is zero

	A	B	C	D	E	F
1	Output (number	Fixed cost (£)	Variable cost (£)	Total cost (£)	Total revenue (£)	Profit (£)
2	of items made)					
3	0	1500	0	1500	0	−1500
4	100	1500	300	1800	600	−200
5	200	1500	600	2100	1200	−900
6	300	1500	900	2400	1800	−600
7	400	1500	1200	2700	2400	−300
8	500	1500	1500	3000	3000	0
9	600	1500	1800	3300	3600	300
10	700	1500	2100	3600	4200	600
11	800	1500	2400	3900	4800	900
12	900	1500	2700	4200	5400	1200
13	1000	1500	3000	4500	6000	1500

The break-even point is where the 'total revenue' and 'total cost' lines cross

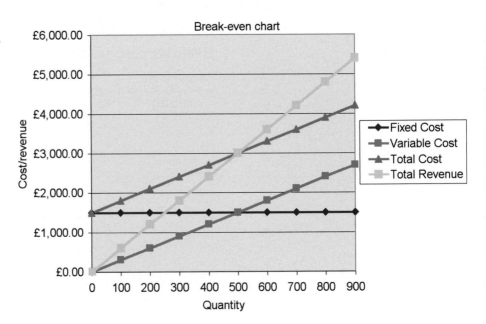

The basic principle is pretty straightforward. The fixed costs have to be paid even if the firm produces nothing. In this case, they come to £1500. The product sells for £6 per unit, but costs £3 to make. So every time the firm sells a product, they have £3 left after paying the variable cost for that item. This money will be used to pay the fixed costs. It will take 500 products to raise the £1500 needed to cover the fixed costs. Any products they sell above 500 will each contribute £3 profit to the firm.

So, another way to calculate the number of products required to reach the break-even point is to use the following formula:

$$\text{break-even output} = \frac{\text{fixed cost}}{\text{contribution per unit of output}}$$

where:

$$\text{contribution} = \text{selling price} - \text{unit cost}$$

If the firm were currently producing and selling 700 products, then it could see sales fall by 200 before it reached the break-even point of 500. This means that it has a **margin of safety** of 200.

$$\text{margin of safety} = \text{current output} - \text{break-even level of output}$$

There are two problems with break-even analysis.

1 It assumes that everything made will be sold. Unsold products will make a loss equal to the variable cost.
2 It assumes that all products can be sold at the same selling price. In practice, firms wishing to increase sales may have to reduce the selling price.

■ *ICT Case study*

Flame's Hairdressers is a small hairdressing salon. The owners have asked you to calculate how many customers they need before they can break even. They have supplied you with the following information.

Average price per customer:	£8
Fixed cost per month:	£2000
Variable cost per hair appointment:	£3

Tasks

1 Calculate how many customers the salon needs each month in order to break even.
2 Use the information provided to draw a break-even chart. Mark on your graph the break-even point. You should get the same break-even point using the two different methods.
3 What will happen to the break-even point if the variable cost increases to £4 per appointment?

■ *ICT Activity*

1 Set up a spreadsheet that will enable you to show the break-even level of output for a business. Your spreadsheet will need the following headings.

- quantity
- fixed cost
- variable cost
- total cost
- total revenue
- total profit

Insert formulas to calculate total cost and total profit. The formulas you need for the other columns will depend on the cost and revenue data.

2 Use your spreadsheet to show the break-even level of output for Flame's Hairdressers, described in the case study on page 119.
   a) Create a graph to illustrate the break-even level of output.
   b) Change your data to show the effect of an increase in variable cost from £3 to £4 per appointment. Create a new graph and mark on it how the break-even point has changed.

19 Production: use of computers to improve design and efficiency

ICT can be used in many ways to improve the efficiency of businesses in both production and in sales and marketing.

Using ICT in production
CAD/CAM

The introduction of computer-aided design (CAD) and computer-aided manufacture (CAM) have made a big difference to the way companies design and make goods (Unit 6). In the past, products were designed in a drawing office, where working drawings were produced by hand, often on the same premises as the manufacturing department. The drawings were passed to the workshop, where engineers would develop a method for producing the required item.

With the advent of CAD, designs can be produced anywhere in the world, often by a specialist firm, and then converted into a computer file. This file can then be e-mailed to the manufacturing company.

Advanced CAD and CAM software means that manufacturing operatives are now usually technicians rather than engineers

When the manufacturer receives the file, it is fed into a computer-controlled manufacturing system, which may comprise either a single machine or a whole production line. The item is then produced. As the file is specifically aimed at controlling the machines in the manufacturing base, little intervention is needed on the part of the engineers. Once the machines have been set up and the materials prepared, the software takes over. This means that the manufacturing base is often staffed by technicians rather than traditional engineers. The practical knowledge of manufacturing has been incorporated into the CAD and CAM software.

This means that the design centre and the manufacturing centre can be in different parts of the world, enabling companies to recruit and train staff in different countries, and often to save money on factory building and staffing costs.

Time management

One of the most costly aspects of supplying any goods or services is time. ICT can be very useful in **time management**, as it can be used to organise operations in an efficient pattern. For example, ICT can be used to set machines to carry out automatic maintenance routines overnight, when they are not being used to manufacture goods. It can also be used to automatically remind telesales staff to attend a meeting, by setting an alarm to appear on the computer monitors of the appropriate staff.

The traditional way for firms to keep tabs on employees' working hours was to have them 'clock in' and 'clock out'. In this way, start and finish times were marked on each worker's timecard

Modern businesses often require all staff to log on to a computer system to start work, rather than 'clock in' in the traditional way. The computer system can then monitor staff work patterns and in some cases adjust payment of wages accordingly. There is also a benefit in knowing where staff are at all times, in case of an emergency.

Work-flow analysis

Work-flow analysis is an extension of time management – ICT is used to ensure that the whole production system, from procurement of materials to dispatch of goods, is organised in an efficient manner. Systems such as 'just in time' (JIT) and 'product streaming' have been developed from this aspect of ICT use.

■ *ICT Case study*

The production of drugs at a multinational drug company is organised using 'product streaming'.

The raw materials arrive at the manufacturing centre and are immediately logged into the computer database. All packages are labelled with a bar code that contains information regarding contents, date and time of delivery, and storage requirements. Robotic trolleys then carry the raw materials to a holding area until they are needed.

As they are needed, the raw materials are automatically transported to the appropriate areas of the production room. Here, mixing equipment is computer-monitored as the raw materials are mixed.

While the tablets are being manufactured, the pre-printed packages are delivered to the packaging department. The tablets are then transported to the packaging area, where they are automatically loaded into machines with the packages. The machine then loads a set number of tablets into each package.

The last stage is to combine a number of packets, now filled with tablets, into cartons, which are then packed onto pallets and deposited ready for dispatch to the distributors.

The majority of the production is completely automatic. The main aspect that requires human workers is the cleaning of the equipment prior to use and the monitoring of the system to ensure that any problems are dealt with before production is hampered.

This system enables the company to produce millions of tablets each month, without having to store raw materials or packaging on site, thereby cutting down the size of the factory and the chance of contamination (accidental mixing of materials). It also means that the workforce has been cut down from large numbers of manual workers to a small band of cleaners and highly-skilled ICT technicians.

Tasks

1 Describe the impact that the 'product streaming' system could have in supermarket stocking and sales.
2 The successful manufacture of a product relies on the correct use of processes and materials. Produce a report on a product that you feel has utilised modern processes and new materials in its manufacture.

Using ICT in sales and marketing

Internet

The use of ICT to improve the areas of sales and marketing has changed dramatically with the advent of the internet. Companies can now search for suppliers of raw materials all over the world. When a supplier has been found, orders can be made and payments organised using e-mail and associated software. This is called **e-procurement**.

In the past, manufacturing companies were contacted by sales representatives from suppliers, and shown samples of materials they might wish to buy. Now, using the internet, a company can search quickly through the websites of dozens of suppliers, and arrange for samples or further information to be sent, completely bypassing the sales force.

Orders can be made over the internet, either through secure internet sites or using e-mail. The orders can then be dispatched and invoices sent for payment much more quickly and efficiently.

Advertising

The use of the internet for advertising via a website means that companies can contact potential customers all over the world (Unit 4). This has lead to some companies broadening their customer base to include regions they would not have been able to reach in the past. For example, pre-packed coffee from a company in the USA is now sold to customers in all corners of the world.

Management of customer data

Because of this broadening of customer base, it has become even more important to store customer details in an organised fashion. The use of databases in this area has proved invaluable to many companies. Millions of customer account details can now be stored in a relatively small area, with quick and easy access. This means that when a new product or service is launched, the details of existing customers can be used to create a mail-merge letter informing them of the launch. This can then be posted to customers or e-mailed direct to their computers.

Section 4 Summary questions

■ 16 Workplace organisation: location and the working environment

1 Explain why a business that sells insurance on the internet faces fewer constraints on where to set up production than an Estate Agent.

2 a) Explain the difference between open-plan and cellular offices.
   b) Which type of office design might be used for the call centre of a large telephone banking business?
   c) Why might some firms use a mixture of open-plan and cellular offices?

3 Sinusbytes is a business that designs and supplies computer systems for offices. It employs 300 core workers and 400 peripheral workers. Explain how working conditions might be different for the two types of worker.

4 What is 'ergonomics'?

■ 17 Workplace organisation: storing and sharing information

1 Explain two problems that could result from a business being unable to keep its computer system secure from hackers or viruses.

2 What is a WAN? Explain how it is different from a LAN.

3 Identify and explain four ways in which a business could prevent unauthorised access to files stored on its computer network.

4 Explain why it is important for employees to change their password at frequent intervals.

5 a) Explain why it is important that a firm makes back-up copies of important files on its computer system.
   b) Where should the back-up files be stored?
   c) When is the best time to make back-up copies of the files?

6 Carla has produced two different versions of an advertisement for a new brand of toothpaste. Give a sensible filename for each of the two files.

7 **a)** What is a 'folder' on a computer?
   b) Why is it a good idea to store computer files inside folders?

8 Most computers store files using a hierarchical system. Explain what this means.

9 What do the initials RAM stand for?

10 Why is it a good idea to save computer work at frequent intervals? Use the term 'RAM' in your answer.

11 Explain why it can be a good idea to give computer files a number of keywords.

■ 18 Production: costs and break-even analysis

1 What are the differences between fixed cost and variable cost?

2 Which of the following costs are likely to be fixed and which variable?

Cost	Fixed or variable?
Wages paid to production workers	
Salaries paid to sales staff	
Purchase of raw materials	
Repaying a loan used to buy the main factory	
Cost of an advertising campaign	

3 A music shop sells CDs at an average price of £12 each. The shop has a fixed cost of £10,000 per month. It has estimated its variable cost to equal £9 per CD.
   a) How many CDs does the shop need to sell each month in order to break even?
   b) What will happen to its break-even point if it raises the price of CDs to £19?
   c) How useful is your answer to **b)**?

4 A car manufacturer has fixed costs of £36 million each year. Each car costs £6,000 to build. 12,000 cars are made in a year. Each car sells for £11,000.
   a) How much is the average cost of making each car?
   b) How many cars need to be sold if the car manufacturer is to break even?

c) Has the firm made a profit if it sells all 12,000 cars?

d) How much profit has it made in total?

e) What is the margin of safety if the firm sells all 12,000 cars?

■ 19 Production: use of computers to improve design and efficiency

1 Describe how CAD and CAM systems can be combined to improve manufacture of a product.

2 Companies now have manufacturing bases all over the world. How has the use of computers helped to enable companies to do this?

3 Describe two ways in which time management can improve the efficiency of a company.

4 Carry out a work-flow analysis of your day. Make a note of where re-organising your time could enable you to do more work, or spend more time relaxing.

5 Explain how a company might benefit from carrying out a work-flow analysis.

6 Find two advertisements for two similar products, one in a newspaper or magazine and one on the internet. Evaluate the advertisements and compare how effective they are in motivating a potential customer to purchase the item.

7 Explain why it is important for companies to keep up-to-date records of sales and customer details.

8 Produce a comparison between traditional methods of filing company records and using a modern database

Section 5

Marketing

20

What is marketing?

Marketing is perhaps the most important activity carried out by a business. Most people think that marketing is simply how the firm advertises its products. Advertising is important but it is only one small part of marketing.

Marketing is the art of trying to make it impossible for the customer not to buy your product!

If you think of some of the reasons why you might *not* buy a particular product, you will begin to see what marketing is all about. You might not buy a particular product because:

- it is not a product that you want to buy
- it is too expensive
- you do not know it exists
- you are unable to find anywhere that sells it
- it has a bad reputation.

Marketing principles

The main features of marketing are summarised in the four Ps – product, price, promotion and place. A **marketing strategy** is the name for a plan to market a product that covers all four Ps.

Product

It is important that the product is one that customers will want to buy. The best way to ensure this, is to find out what customers want, and then make it for them. It is best if the product has something that makes it different to those made by your competitors. This is called product differentiation. The product is then said to have a unique selling proposition or **USP**. The USP might be something that is emphasised when the product is promoted.

Price

The price charged should offer the customer good value for money. Note that this does not mean that the product must be cheap. If the customer can be made to think that the product is better than the others on the market, they might be persuaded to pay extra for it. This may earn the business greater profit. Getting the customer to pay a higher price for a better product is called 'adding value'.

Promotion

Promotion includes all the different ways that the product can be brought to the customer's attention.

The most well-known method is advertising. Advertising can be very expensive. TV advertising campaigns can cost millions of pounds.

Point of sale promotions draw the customer's attention to a product

Another very popular method is called 'point-of-sale' promotion. This is where the firm puts eye-catching display cases for its products in the shops where the product is sold.

Place

'Place' describes the various outlets from which the customer can buy the product. In recent years, the biggest growth area has been on-line retailing. This means that nowadays most firms can make their products available for sale in people's homes.

Meeting the need

The most important principle with the four Ps is that each P must be consistent with the others. It is no use having a quality product, advertised in quality newspapers and available in quality retail outlets if the product is sold too cheaply. If the price is too low, people may not believe that it is a quality product.

Marketing is therefore about identifying customer needs and making products available that meet those needs. So firms need to carry out **market research** in order to find out what the customer wants. In Unit 21, we focus on how ICT can be used to obtain and analyse market research data.

■ *ICT Case study*

The marketing of sports equipment to teenagers can be seen as an example of the 4Ps.

A high street shop wanted to promote a new range of football clothing and boots. They decide to direct their marketing at teenagers, as they were the most likely to be involved in the purchases of the goods.

The first P – Product, was football clothing and boots, these were known to be popular with the chosen client group. To advertise the product the company decided to produce a glossy brochure, with lots of high quality photographs of well-known footballers wearing the items that would be available for sale in their shops.

The second P – Price, was also considered, the goods were relatively expensive, building a certain feeling of quality! Famous company logos were incorporated, again reflecting quality. The advertising campaign was also expensive, but the company expected it to be successful, so they were willing to invest in it.

The third P – Promotion, involved getting endorsements from famous players, and well-known brand names. These appeared in the brochure, helping to develop the aspirational impact of the goods. Teenagers who wanted to be able to play as well as their heroes, or at least look like them, would be more willing to pay slightly higher prices if they thought they were getting the *real* thing.

The fourth P – Place, involved delivering and distributing the brochures to pupils in schools near the shops. The brochures carried addresses of the local shops.

Results: due to the targeting, the campaign was extremely successful. 91% of students said they were likely to visit a particular store when they wanted to purchase one of these products.

Tasks

1 Supermarkets use the position of a product to help to sell it – take a look around your local supermarket and identify three products that are positioned in a way that helps to influence people to purchase them.
2 Produce a report on an advertising campaign that you think is successful.
3 Describe two advantages of using ICT to help advertise a product.

21

Marketing: research and strategy

There are two main types of market research, described in the following paragraphs.

Desk research

Desk research is also known as secondary research. This is where the business uses data that has already been obtained by other organisations. An example would be the use of a survey carried out by a specialist market research agency.

A benefit of using desk research is that the data already exists. Obtaining the information is likely to cost the firm less than if it produced it itself. A problem with secondary data is that it might be out of date. Also, the data might not be completely relevant to the particular needs of the business.

Field research

Field research is also known as primary research. This is where the firm carries out its own research. The most common method is to use a questionnaire to ask people for their opinions. Similar to questionnaires are panel interviews and focus groups. These allow the researcher to find out detailed information from a small group of people.

The best way to find out is to ask!

Questionnaires are a good way of obtaining **quantitative** information. This is information that is based on facts and can be measured. For example, the question 'How many cans of soft drink do you buy each week?' would give a quantitative answer.

ICT can be used to generate the questionnaires. The results can then be collected and entered into a spreadsheet for analysis. The spreadsheet can be used to create graphs of the most interesting results, which can be exported into a publishing or presentation program to produce the market research report.

Panel interviews and focus groups are a good way of obtaining **qualitative** information. This is information about people's feelings and opinions. For example, the question 'Why do you buy soft drinks and not tea or coffee?' would give a qualitative answer.

In recent years, ICT has made a number of changes to the way that firms are able to carry out field research.

Loyalty cards

Loyalty cards allow the company to collect detailed information about customers' shopping habits. In return, the customer collects 'reward points' at each shopping visit

Many supermarkets and other large retailers use **loyalty cards**. Customers use the card each time they make a purchase. The checkout bar-code scanner records the exact details of each product the customer buys. The loyalty card contains details about the customer that are also stored on the firm's customer database.

The effect of this is that the shop is able to determine exactly what each customer has purchased. This can be analysed in order to determine the customer's shopping habits. For example, the database could record that a certain customer buys dog biscuits, but doesn't buy any other products for their dog. The supermarket could then send that customer details of special offers for dog food.

Internet cookies

Every time a person opens a new internet website, the website will send a small text file to the person's computer. The text file contains information that the website can recognise the next time the person visits it. These text files are called **cookies**. They are named after fortune cookies.

Cookies can be used by a company to find out how many people visit its website and how often they make return visits.

■ *ICT Activity*

You work as a marketing assistant for Chumpo Chocolates Ltd. Chumpo Chocolates used to be the UK's biggest producer of sweets and snack foods. In recent years, their sales have suffered as other manufacturers have become more competitive.

You have been asked to develop a new product that will send Chumpo Chocolates back to the top of the market.

Tasks

1 Carry out some secondary research into what other manufacturers are producing. You could use the internet to help you find this information.
2 Produce a questionnaire and use it to find out what products might be successful.
3 Analyse the results of your questionnaire. Produce graphs of any interesting or useful results (Units 2 and 3).
4 Produce a marketing strategy for your product. Make sure that you cover all the four Ps (Unit 20). As part of your strategy, you could use image-creation software (Unit 6) to create a design for your packaging.
5 Put all this together into a multimedia presentation (Unit 5). Give a presentation to the rest of the class about your product and its marketing strategy.

Business operates within a global society. Increased travel means that more and more people are aware of places and cultures in different parts of the world. Improvements in technology, such as the internet and satellite communications, mean that information can be transmitted around the world in seconds. Firms increasingly advertise their products on the internet and global satellite television channels.

Some brands are truly international – they are recognised instantly all over the world

These changes are transforming the way that we live and work. They are also changing the way that firms market their products. Large businesses tend to market their products on a global scale. Often the same product is sold all over the world, using the same brand name and using the same advertising methods. Sometimes the marketing is adapted to meet particular local needs. These changes often reflect religious or cultural differences.

Firms who manufacture products in more than one country are called **multinational** firms. These firms make much use of wide area networks (WANs). The WAN enables data to be transferred between different parts of the firm's global computer system.

Benefits of a global market

Globalisation is said to have a number of benefits.

- One benefit is that successful businesses can expand into new markets and become much bigger. Bigger firms often have **economies of scale**. These are the cost savings that come from operating on a large scale. Such cost savings can be passed on to the consumer in the form of lower prices.
- Globalisation should also increase the amount of choice for consumers. Products produced in one part of the world can be made available to consumers in other places. This is especially true of businesses that trade on the internet.

Drawbacks of a global market

However, some people are not convinced that globalisation is a good thing. They point to a number of problems.

■ Large multinational firms have a lot of economic power. They might use their economies of scale to charge prices that force smaller firms out of the market. This will give the multinationals the market power needed to raise prices. So the economies of scale may simply result in higher profits, instead of lower prices for consumers.

■ If the world ends up with a small number of large multinationals, then the amount of choice may be limited. Critics point to the brewing industry as an example. At the beginning of the 19th century, there were hundreds of small breweries in the UK. Today there are a handful of large breweries. Some of these are part of multinational businesses. In the future there may be fewer still.

■ Sometimes, although consumers may seem to have a choice, this choice is more apparent than real. For example, in a typical UK 'High Street' a number of seemingly different clothing and electrical goods stores are in fact all owned by the same firms. In a supermarket, there may appear to be a range of differently branded breakfast cereals or washing powders, for example, but in fact they are all made by the same manufacturers.

■ *ICT Activity*

You work as a journalist for the *Freshley Gazette*, the biggest-selling quality local newspaper in the Freshley area.

You have been asked to prepare an article for the newspaper on the effects of globalisation.

Tasks

1 Carry out some research for your article. For example, you could ask friends and family whether globalisation has affected them and whether they think it is a good idea.
2 If possible, carry out some research on the internet. For example, you could look at other newspaper articles that have been written on this subject.
3 When you have completed your research, write the article using publishing software.

Section 5 Summary questions

Work through these questions to check your knowledge of each unit.

■ 20 What is marketing?

1 List the four Ps of a good marketing strategy.

2 Explain why it is important to find out what consumers want from a product.

3 What is a USP? Explain why all products should have one.

4 Why can it be a bad idea to make the price of a product too low?

5 Explain what is meant by 'point of sale' promotion.

6 How is the internet changing the 'place' where products are sold?

■ 21 Marketing: research and strategy

1 Explain the difference between desk research and field research.

2 Give two benefits and two drawbacks of using desk research.

3 Give one benefit and one drawback of using field research.

4 A manufacturer of breakfast cereals wishes to carry out some market research into what its customers think of its products. It is unsure whether to use a questionnaire or a focus group.
   a) Explain the difference between these two market research methods.
   b) If you had to pick just one method, which one would you recommend, and why?
   c) Why might it be a good idea to use both methods?

5 What is a loyalty card? How can loyalty cards be used to collect information on customer shopping behaviour?

6 What is an internet cookie? What information can cookies give the owner of a website?

■ 22 International communications

1 Explain why marketing is increasingly being carried out on a global scale.

2 Explain why, despite this, firms still need to pay attention to local markets.

3 Explain how the internet is accelerating the moves towards a global economy.

4 Explain two benefits of globalisation for business.

5 Explain two benefits of globalisation for consumers.

6 Explain three drawbacks of globalisation for consumers.

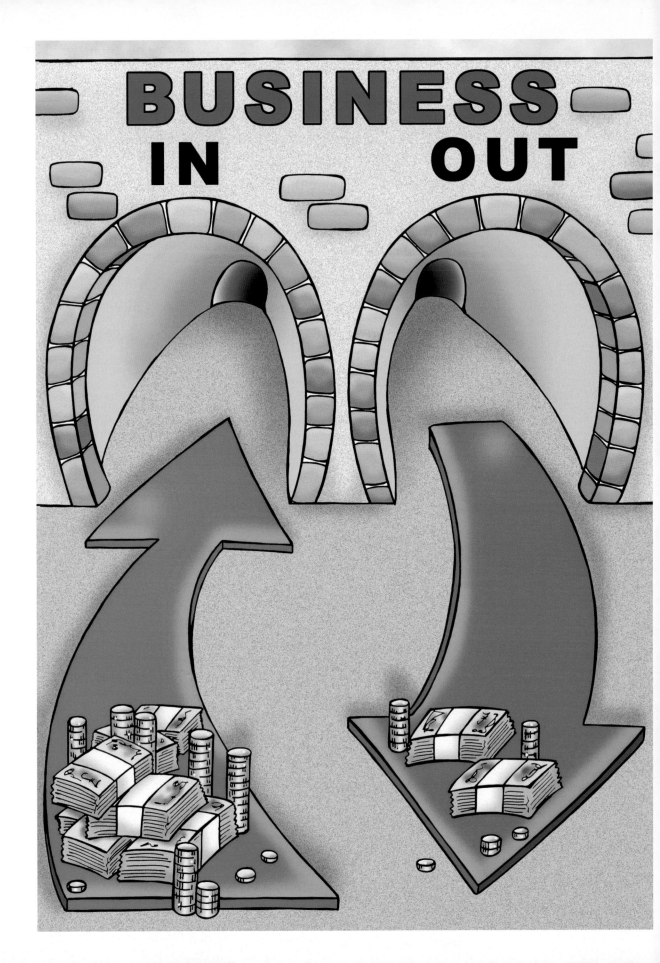

Section 6

Finance

In this unit, and the following Unit 24, we look at two of the most important issues that businesses have to manage – profits and cash flow.

Profits are the rewards given to the people who have invested in the business. They are the difference between the firm's income and its expenses.

Cash flow is the money that flows into and out of the business on a daily basis. It is needed to pay the firm's bills. It is possible for a profitable business to fail if it does not have enough cash at the right times.

Cash flow

There are a number of reasons why firms can run out of money and so face cash flow problems.

Sources of cash flow problems

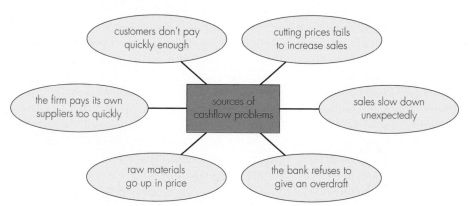

If a firm does not have enough cash to pay its debts it could be ordered by a Court of Law to sell some of its assets to raise the cash. This could result in the business being unable to continue trading. Poor cash flow management is the most common reason why businesses cease trading.

In order to try to spot any potential cash flow problems, firms produce a **cash flow forecast**. These are normally produced for the coming six or twelve months. An example for a company called Anyfirm is shown below.

	A	B	C	D	E	F	G	H	I	J	K	L	M	N
1	**Cash Flow Forecast Anyfirm**													
2		January	February	March	April	May	June	July	August	September	October	November	December	Total
3	Receipts													
4	Loans	£5,000												£5,000
5	Sales	£3,000	£3,000	£6,000	£6,000	£6,000	£8,000	£8,000	£8,000	£6,000	£6,000	£6,000	£4,000	£70,000
6	Total Receipts (A)	£8,000	£3,000	£6,000	£6,000	£6,000	£8,000	£8,000	£8,000	£6,000	£6,000	£6,000	£4,000	£75,000
7														
8	Payments													
9	Delivery van		£8,000											£8,000
10	Materials	£600	£1,200	£1,200	£1,200	£2,400	£2,400	£2,400	£1,200	£1,200	£1,200	£1,200	£1,200	£17,400
11	Production worker wages	£500	£500	£500	£500	£500	£500	£1,100	£1,100	£1,100	£1,100	£500	£500	£8,400
12	Office salaries	£300	£300	£300	£300	£300	£300	£500	£500	£500	£500	£300	£300	£4,400
13	Loan repayments	£250	£250	£250	£250	£250	£250	£250	£250	£250	£250	£250	£250	£3,000
14	Other expenses	£2,000	£2,000	£2,000	£2,000	£2,500	£2,500	£2,500	£2,500	£2,500	£2,500	£2,500	£2,500	£28,000
15	Total Payments (B)	£3,650	£12,250	£4,250	£4,250	£5,950	£5,950	£6,750	£5,550	£5,550	£5,550	£4,750	£4,750	£69,200
16														£0
17	Opening balance (C)	£0	£4,350	-£4,900	-£3,150	-£1,400	-£1,350	£700	£1,950	£4,400	£4,850	£5,300	£6,550	£0
18	Receipts (A) - Payments (B)	£4,350	-£9,250	£1,750	£1,750	£50	£2,050	£1,250	£2,450	£450	£450	£1,250	-£750	£5,800
19	Closing balance (C + (A - B))	£4,350	-£4,900	-£3,150	-£1,400	-£1,350	£700	£1,950	£4,400	£4,850	£5,300	£6,550	£5,800	£5,800

Anyfirm's cash flow
forecast for twelve
months (showing figures)

	A	B	C	D	E	F	G	H	I	J	K	L	M	N
1	Cash Flow Forecast Anyfirm													
2		January	February	March	April	May	June	July	August	September	October	November	December	Total
3	Receipts													
4	Loans	5000												=SUM(B4:M4)
5	Sales	3000	3000	6000	6000	6000	8000	8000	8000	6000	6000	6000	4000	=SUM(B5:M5)
6	Total Receipts (A)	=SUM(B4:B5)	=SUM(C4:C5)	=SUM(D4:D5)	=SUM(E4:E5)	=SUM(F4:F5)	=SUM(G4:G5)	=SUM(H4:H5)	=SUM(I4:I5)	=SUM(J4:J5)	=SUM(K4:K5)	=SUM(L4:L5)	=SUM(M4:M5)	=SUM(B6:M6)
7														
8	Payments													
9	Delivery van		8000											=SUM(B9:M9)
10	Materials	600	1200	1200	1200	2400	2400	2400	1200	1200	1200	1200	1200	=SUM(B10:M10)
11	Production worker wages	500	500	500	500	500	500	1100	1100	1100	1100	500	500	=SUM(B11:M11)
12	Office salaries	300	300	300	300	300	300	500	500	500	500	300	300	=SUM(B12:M12)
13	Loan repayments	250	250	250	250	250	250	250	250	250	250	250	250	=SUM(B13:M13)
14	Other expenses	2000	2000	2000	2000	2500	2500	2500	2500	2500	2500	2500	2500	=SUM(B14:M14)
15	Total Payments (B)	=SUM(B9:B14)	=SUM(C9:C14)	=SUM(D9:D14)	=SUM(E9:E14)	=SUM(F9:F14)	=SUM(G9:G14)	=SUM(H9:H14)	=SUM(I9:I14)	=SUM(J9:J14)	=SUM(K9:K14)	=SUM(L9:L14)	=SUM(M9:M14)	=SUM(B15:M15)
16														=SUM(B16:M16)
17	Opening balance (C)	0	=B19	=C19	=D19	=E19	=F19	=G19	=H19	=I19	=J19	=K19	=L19	=B17
18	Receipts (A) - Payments (B)	=B6-B15	=C6-C15	=D6-D15	=E6-E15	=F6-F15	=G6-G15	=H6-H15	=I6-I15	=J6-J15	=K6-K15	=L6-L15	=M6-M15	=N6-N15
19	Closing balance (C + (A - B))	=SUM(B17:B18)	=SUM(C17:C18)	=SUM(D17:D18)	=SUM(E17:E18)	=SUM(F17:F18)	=SUM(G17:G18)	=SUM(H17:H18)	=SUM(I17:I18)	=SUM(J17:J18)	=SUM(K17:K18)	=SUM(L17:L18)	=SUM(M17:M18)	=SUM(N17:N18)

Anyfirm's cash flow
forecast for twelve
months (showing
formulas)

In this example, Anyfirm is going to have a cash flow problem
between February and May. But in general its cash flow looks quite
healthy. As a result it could probably convince its bank to give it an
overdraft for the first six months of the year.

Producing a cash flow forecast

A good way to produce a cash flow forecast is to use a spreadsheet
model. The first step is to create a template. This will include all the
headings plus the formulas that can be used to automatically
calculate the receipts, payments and the cash balance. Once the
template has been saved the firm can enter its figures and calculate
the cash balance.

One benefit of using a spreadsheet is that the firm can carry out
'what-if analysis' (Unit 2). The owners could change some of the
figures to see how they might be able to avoid a cash flow problem.

■ *ICT Activity 1*

Set up a blank spreadsheet template that can be used to create a cash flow forecast. Use the 'Anyfirm' example above to help you set out the spreadsheet.

1 Write formulas that will automatically insert the following information:

- ■ total cash received
- ■ total payments made
- ■ opening balance of each month (from month 2 onwards)
- ■ total cash received minus total payments made
- ■ closing bank balance

2 Use the 'copy formula' function so that you only have to write each formula once.

3 Use text formatting to improve the appearance of your spreadsheet.

4 Print a copy of your spreadsheet displaying the formulas.

5 Enter the data from the 'Anyfirm' example above. Make sure that your spreadsheet produces the same, correct, closing bank balance for each month.

■ *ICT Activity 2*

Bob Dixon, a self-employed builder, has asked you to prepare a cash flow forecast for his business, for the next year. Bob has supplied you with the following information.

Details of Bob's Building Business

- I expect to receive £5,000 each month from January to March. I expect sales will be £9,000 each month in April and May, then £11,000 each month from June to September. It will then fall to £8,000 each month in October and November, and then £5,000 in December.
- I employ two builders, who I will pay £1000 each, per month. I expect that this will go up to £1,500 each, per month, from May to September.
- I employ a part-time office manager, who I pay £800 per month.
- I estimate that my spending on raw materials will be equal to 30% of my monthly sales income.
- I have general business expenses of £400 per month but from February to September I will be spending £200 per month advertising in the local papers.
- In May I will need to buy a new van. This will cost £10,000. I will be taking out a loan of £8,000 in May to help cover this. I will begin paying this back in June at £500 each month.
- I pay my insurance every three months, starting in March. The annual cost is £900.
- I will be making a withdrawal of £1,800 each month. This will cover my own wages.

Tasks

1 Adapt your existing spreadsheet template and use it to create a cash flow forecast for Bob.

2 Comment on the figures.

3 Bob has asked you to try to give him some advice on how he can improve his expected cash flow next year. Experiment by changing some of the figures and see the effect on cash flow. For example, could Bob pay his builders less? Does he need an office assistant? Could he pay himself less? Could he increase his sales? Could he reduce his raw material costs to 25% of sales?

4 Write Bob a short report explaining how he could improve his cash flow next year. Give him some suggestions as to what he could change and what the effects would be. Comment on your suggestions. For example, how practical are your suggestions? Might they cause problems for the way that the business operates?

24 Profit and loss account

In Unit 23, we saw that a cash flow forecast is a way of making a prediction about the future of a business. The profit and loss account, by contrast, looks back on the previous year's trading. It is a record of whether or not the firm made any profit from its trading activities.

The profit and loss account is made up of three different sections. An example is shown below.

Profit and loss account for Anyfirm (showing figures)

	A	B	C
1	Trading, Profit and Loss Account for Anyfirm		
2		£	£
3	Revenue		70000
4	less Cost of Sales		
5	Opening Stock	5000	
6	Purchases	17400	
7	Production worker wages	8400	
8		30800	
9	Less Closing Stock	7000	
10			23800
11	Gross Profit		46200
12	less expenses		
13	Office salaries	4400	
14	Loan repayments	3000	
15	Other expenses	28000	
16			35400
17	Profit before taxation (Net Profit)		10800
18			
19	Taxation		2160
20	Dividends		5184
21	Retained Profit		3456

Profit and loss account for Anyfirm (showing formulas)

	A	B	C
1	Trading, Profit and Loss Account for Anyfirm		
2		£	£
3	Revenue		70000
4	less Cost of Sales		
5	Opening Stock	5000	
6	Purchases	17400	
7	Production worker wages	8400	
8		=SUM(B5:B7)	
9	Less Closing Stock	7000	
10			=B8-B9
11	Gross Profit		=C3-C10
12	less expenses		
13	Office salaries	4400	
14	Loan repayments	3000	
15	Other expenses	28000	
16			=SUM(B13:B15)
17	Profit before taxation (Net Profit)		=C11-C16
18			
19	Taxation		=C17*0.2
20	Dividends		=(C17-C19)*0.6
21	Retained Profit		=(C17-C19)*0.4

A profit and loss account is an important way of assessing a company's performance

The trading account

The trading account tells the firm if it has made any profit through making and selling its products. It records the difference between the income received from selling the product and the variable (direct) cost of making it (Unit 18).

The account has to record the cost of the products actually sold during the year. Some of these products will have been made using stock bought in the previous year. At the end of the year some stock will be left over. This stock will be used to make next year's products. So the firm has to make an adjustment called 'cost of sales' to reflect this.

cost of sales = opening stock + variable cost − closing stock

The difference between the firm's revenue and its variable costs is called **gross profit**.

Profit and loss account

This is the part that gives the whole account its name. In this section the gross profit is used to pay for all the firm's general business expenses – in other words, its fixed (indirect) costs.

As well as selling their main products, some firms will have other sources of income. These include renting out property or income from investments such as shares. This income is shown in the profit and loss section.

The difference between the firm's gross profit and its general business expenses is called **net profit**.

Appropriation account

This is the final section. It records what happens to the net profit. There are three main ways that the net profit will be used.

1 Taxation

The government takes a share of the net profit made by any business. This is why net profit is sometimes called 'profit before taxation'.

2 Dividends to shareholders

This is the proportion of the profit after tax that the business decides to give to the **shareholders**. The **dividend** is the shareholders' reward for investing in the company.

3 Retained profit

This is what remains of the net profit after the government and shareholders have received their share. It is normally used to purchase the assets that the business needs in order to operate – for example, vehicles, machinery and computer systems.

If the **shareholders** decide that the dividend payment is too small they may decide to sell their shares to someone else. This is one way that business ownership can change hands. For this reason many firms find themselves under pressure to pay a high dividend. This might mean that there are not enough retained profits to buy the assets that the business needs.

Producing a profit and loss account

A simple way to produce a profit and loss account is to use a spreadsheet. The steps involved are the same as for producing the cash flow forecast (Unit 23). In fact, it is possible to link the two worksheets together – the numbers on the profit and loss account can be taken directly from the cash flow sheet. In this way, the firm can see the impact of its 'what-if analysis' on the likely level of profit. The firm can also look at the impact of giving different amounts of dividends on the level of retained profit.

▪ *ICT Activity 1*

Produce a spreadsheet template that you can use to calculate a profit and loss account. Use the 'Anyfirm' example on page 146 to help you lay out your spreadsheet.

Tasks

1 Write formulas to enable you to calculate automatically the following things:

- cost of sales
- gross profit
- total expenses
- net profit

2 Print a copy of your spreadsheet showing the formulas.
3 Enter the information from the 'Anyfirm Profit and Loss Account' onto your spreadsheet. Make sure that *your* spreadsheet produces the same, correct, profit figures.

■ *ICT Activity 2*

RDS Sports Limited owns a chain of sports shops in Yorkshire and Lancashire. Jane Sibley, the Finance Director, has asked you to produce the business's profit and loss account for the year 2001 to 2002. She has supplied you with the following information.

**Information about RDS Sport
in 2001 to 2002**

- Our sales income was £958,000.
- We bought stock worth £220,000.
- At the start of the year, we had £35,000 of stock.
  This had risen to £39,000 at the end of the year.
- We paid out £240,000 in wages to our shop workers. We paid salaries totalling £250,000 to our office staff. Our other office expenses were £164,000.
- We made repayments of £30,000 on a bank loan.
- We had to pay 20% of our net profit as taxation to the government. We split the rest of the profit equally between our shareholders and retained profit.

Task

Create RDS Sports' profit and loss account. You should use a spreadsheet. You could adapt the spreadsheet you created in *ICT Activity 1*, on page 149. Add formulas so that the spreadsheet will divide up the net profit in the 'appropriation' part of the account.

■ *ICT Activity 3 – extension*

It is possible to link two or more spreadsheets together. Formulas in one worksheet can make use of data found in another sheet. For example, the formula C5 = 'Cash flow'!B6*2 means that cell C5 will be equal to the data found in cell B6 of a worksheet called 'Cash flow', multiplied by two.

Task

Produce a profit and loss account for Bob Dixon that links to your cash flow forecast spreadsheet for his business (Unit 23). Most software packages allow you to have both worksheets in the same file. All the information to produce the profit and loss account can be found from the total figures for each item. The only additional information you need is Bob's opening and closing stock. This will enable you to calculate the cost of sales.

- opening stock = £2,500   ■ closing stock = £2,900

How much profit is Bob predicted to make at the end of the year?

Banking services

Throughout this book, we have looked at ways that businesses are making increasing use of ICT. In this unit, we look at one area of business in detail.

Banks have always needed to store data. The very first banks needed to keep accurate records of how much money their customers had deposited with them and how much money they were owed by the people to whom they had given loans.

In the 1960s, banks were among the first businesses to make use of large computer systems to store customer records. Today they are still at the forefront of ICT developments as they make increasing use of internet and digital television technology.

Making payments and transfers

People with bank accounts have a number of different ways that they can pay for goods and services.

Cash and cheques

During most of the 20th century, **cash** and **cheques** were the main payment methods used. Cash is still used but mainly to pay for inexpensive products such as newspapers and sweets. A cheque is an instruction to the customer's bank to allow the business to take money out of the customer's bank account. To be valid, it has to be signed by the customer.

In the past few years, debit cards and credit cards have become increasingly common and cheques are used less often.

Cheques must be properly completed to be valid

Debit cards

Using a debit card (specimen cards above) is much more convenient than writing a cheque, for the customer

A **debit card** is a plastic card that, when used, enables the customer to transfer money from their bank account to the shop's bank account. On the front of the card are printed details of the customer's bank account. These include:

- name of the bank
- **sort code** – the code given to the bank by the database that transfers money from one bank to another
- customer's bank account number – this is the key field in the bank's customer database
- expiry date – after this date, the card cannot be used and must be replaced.

On the back of the debit card is a magnetic stripe. The stripe contains the same details that are printed on the front of the card. It also contains additional information, such as the cardholder's personal identification number (**PIN**). This is a secret four-digit code that only the cardholder should know. It can be used to verify that the person using the card is the cardholder. This helps to reduce the risk of card fraud.

A debit card enables money to be transferred from the customer's bank account straight away.

Credit cards

Credit cards (specimen cards below) can be used to borrow money, but the rates of interest charged are higher than for most other types of loan

A **credit card** looks and works rather like a debit card. It contains similar information. The one important difference is that the money is taken not from the customer's bank account but from the credit card company's account. At the end of the month, the credit card company sends the customer a bill. The credit company gives the customer up to a month to pay the bill. If it is not paid in full within this time the customer is charged interest.

Cash machines

Banks also enable customers to withdraw cash using a cash card. These are often combined with a debit card. To withdraw cash from their bank account, the customer puts the card into a cash machine. The machine reads the magnetic stripe and asks the customer to enter their PIN using a keypad. The cash machine verifies that the correct PIN has been used, and that the customer has sufficient funds in the bank account. The machine then counts out the requested amount of cash and dispenses it to the customer. It then sends an instruction to the customer's bank to reduce their bank balance by the amount withdrawn.

Because these machines count the money automatically, they are also known as automatic telling machines (**ATMs**) – 'teller' is the American word for a bank clerk.

ATMs mean that customers can get cash from their accounts at any time of the day or night

Electronic transfer of funds

'Electronic funds transfer' is usually abbreviated to **EFT**. This is the name given to all payments that are made by transferring money directly from one bank account to another.

When debit or credit cards are used in shops to make a purchase, it is known as 'electronic funds transfer at the point of sale', or EFTPOS for short.

As well as card payments, another method of transferring funds automatically is to set up a **standing order**. This is an instruction to transfer a set amount at a specific time. For example, a standing order could be set up to pay car insurance in 12 monthly instalments.

Businesses can also use EFT to pay their employees. This means that the firm does not need to withdraw large amounts of cash, or write cheques. Using EFT therefore helps to reduce office expenses. Some bank computer systems only update customers' account details at the end of the working day. This is called **batch processing**, because the computer stores all the transactions and then processes them all at the same time. In recent years, some banks have introduced **real-time processing**. This means that the customer's account is updated as the transaction is made.

Real-time processing is more expensive than batch processing because it requires that the computer dedicates more time and memory to processing. But it enables the bank to keep more accurate records of customer accounts.

Telebanking

Telebanking is a general term used to describe the ability to access your bank account without having to visit the bank in person – for example, via the telephone, the internet or digital television.

The main issue associated with telebanking, for the banks and for their customers, is data security. To prevent unauthorised and fraudulent use of accounts, banks use a number of security measures. The most common method is to require customers to give usernames and passwords before access to their account is granted. Such passwords must, of course, be kept secret.

Telephone banking

Instead of visiting a bank branch, the customer telephones a call centre. The operator accesses the customer's bank account and inputs the commands needed to process the payments. Most telephone banks provide a 24-hour service for 365 days of the year. So, for example, a customer could check their bank balance at 3.00 am on New Year's Day!

Internet banking

Customers can visit the bank's website and view their own bank account details. The system works in a similar way to telephone banking. The only difference is that the customers can input the commands themselves via the internet. The bank will use data encryption to send data across the internet. This means that anyone intercepting the data will be unable to decode it and use it.

Digital-television banking

This works in the same way as internet banking. The only difference is that the data is transferred along the digital cable used to carry the television signal, rather than along a telephone line.

The cash-less society

There are a number of proposed benefits associated with the decreased use of cash.

■ As people carry less cash, there is less opportunity for thieves to steal it from them.
■ Banks will require fewer branches as they rely more on call centres and computer networks. This will help to reduce the costs of operating a banking service. This should make customers financially better off.
■ People will be able to make purchases without needing to withdraw cash. It will be easier to make 'impulse purchases'.

However, there are also a number of drawbacks.

■ Card fraud could increase. Thieves may prefer to steal a cash card, which could be used to withdraw several hundred pounds from a bank account, than to steal cash itself.
■ Fraudulent use of credit card details can be used to purchase goods on the internet.
■ As fewer branches are needed, banks will be able to employ fewer people. As a result unemployment among bank staff could increase.

Work through these questions to check your knowledge of each unit.

23 Cash flow forecasting

1   What is the difference between cash flow and profit?

2   Give three reasons why a profitable business might suffer from cash flow problems.

3   Explain, in your own words, how a cash flow forecast is constructed.

4   Give two reasons why the actual cash flow figures for a business might turn out to be different to its cash flow forecast.

5   A bakery produces a cash flow forecast and discovers that it is likely to face a cash flow shortfall for six of the next nine months. Explain three actions that the bakery owners could take in response to this information.

6   Give three benefits to a business of using a spreadsheet to construct its cash flow forecast.

24 Profit and loss account

1   Over what period of time is the profit and loss account calculated?

2   What is calculated in the trading account?

3   In its last financial year, Blands Biscuits buys raw materials worth £250,000. At the start of the year, its opening stock was £25,000. At the end of the year its closing stock was £32,000. Calculate its cost of sales.

4   What is calculated in the profit and loss account?

5   Blands Biscuits made a gross profit of £120,000. Its general business expenses were £105,000. The firm also received an income of £2,000 from shares it owns in other businesses. Calculate the firm's net profit.

6   What information is recorded in the appropriation account?

7   Plackard Signs Ltd. makes a net profit of £60,000. It pays 20% tax to the government and decides to give shareholders 60% of what is left. How much is the firm's retained profit?

8 Explain three benefits to a business of using a spreadsheet to calculate its profit and loss figures.

■ 25 Banking services

1 Identify three pieces of information that have to be written onto a cheque by the account holder.

2 Explain the difference between a debit card and a credit card.

3 Describe the steps involved in withdrawing cash from an automated telling machine.

4 Explain two benefits to businesses of using EFT or EFTPOS.

5 Which method of processing, batch or real-time, will result in payments being deducted from a customer's bank account most quickly?

6 Identify and explain two methods of telebanking.

7 Explain two ways that banks can reduce the risk of unauthorised access to a person's telebank account.

8 What are the main benefits of telebanking for customers and banks?

9 What are the main problems with telebanking?

10 How will payments be made in a cash-less society?

11 Give three benefits of a cash-less society.

12 Give two drawbacks of a cash-less society.

Mouse	A device used to control a computer by moving the cursor, pointing at and selecting icons
Multimedia	A document, presentation or web page, which makes use of more than one communications medium. For example, text, pictures, sound and moving images
Multinational	A business which has branches in more than one country. Multinationals will typically sell their products in more countries than they produce them in
Net pay	The money paid to an employee after deductions such as income tax and national insurance contributions have been removed
Net profit	The amount of profit made by a business after taxation and other expenses have been deducted
Objective	Something that a business intends to achieve. Most objectives are linked to the main aim of making a profit
Open-plan office	An office with no walls between workstations or desks
Operative	An employee who carries out routine tasks and has no management responsibility for the work of others in the business
Password	A string of letters and numbers used to identify a user to a computer
Picture-frame	Area of a document set aside to accept image data. May be moved or resized
Piece rate	Payment to an employee based on the number of items of work done
PIN – personal identification number	A four-digit number used to identify a card-holder when withdrawing money from an automatic telling machine
Pixel	The smallest component of a picture image. The more pixels in an image, the greater will be its clarity and resolution
Presentation	A communication given by one person to a group of people. Can be accompanied by slides produced using presentation software
Process	The manipulation of data so that new data is created. For example, adding two numbers together or increasing the font size of a string of text
Productivity level	The number of items produced per person or over a given period of time
Profit	The difference between the income earned by a business and the cost of running the business
Psychometric test	A test designed to provide information about a person's suitability for a job, based on their personal qualities
Qualitative	Research data which is based on people's feelings and opinions, not hard facts
Quantitative	Research data based on facts, not people's feelings and opinions
RAM – random access memory	The part of a computer's memory which holds data which is currently being used. RAM data needs to be transferred to a permanent memory storage device if a permanent record of the data is needed
Real-time processing	When computer data is processed quickly so that it is able to influence events in the real world

Record	A group of related data all describing the same individual or object. In a database, a record will be divided into a number of different fields
Recruitment	The process of selecting the right person to be appointed to fill a particular vacancy
Relational database	A database which contains a number of separate but linked data tables
Revenue	The money earned by a firm from selling its products
Salary	A fixed payment paid to an employee, usually a fixed rate per year. Not directly related to any unit of work done
Search engine	Software which will look for identified keywords in a database or on the world wide web
Shareholder	A person who has part ownership of a limited company. The number of shares owned determines the proportion of the business which is owned
Software	Programs containing instructions to enable the user to interact with a computer
Sort code	A unique number used on cheques and elsewhere to identify a particular bank
Spreadsheet	A table of data which can be manipulated using formulas
Stakeholder	A person or organisation which has an interest in the performance of a particular business
Standing order	An instruction to a bank to make a regular payment from your bank account to another bank account
State pension	The payment made by the state to people who have reached the national retirement age and are eligible, having paid sufficient national insurance contributions whilst working. Usually paid weekly until death
Supervisor	An operative who has some responsibility for ensuring that other operatives carry out the work required by a manager
Take-home pay	See net pay
Taxable income	The amount of an employee's earnings, which may be taxed by the government. The amount of taxable income is the difference between the person's gross pay and their tax-free allowance
Tax-free allowance	The first part of a person's earnings which is not taxed by the government. People whose gross income is less than their tax-free allowance will pay no income tax
Teamworking	A method of organising production where a group of workers share responsibility for their joint performance
Teleworking	A situation where someone works in a different location to his or her employers. Most teleworkers work from home
Template	A computer file which contains the basic layout needed to produce another document
Text-frame	Area of a document set aside to accept text data. May be moved or resized
Text-message	A message containing written words sent from one mobile phone to another
Time management	Making the best use of one's time. Usually done by putting tasks in order of priority
Time rate	Payment to an employee based on the amount of time taken to complete a task

Unit cost	The cost of producing each of a firm's products. Calculated by dividing the total cost by the number produced
URL – uniform resource locator	The address needed to connect the user's computer with a website
Username	The login identity used by an individual to gain access to data stored on a computer network. Usernames may be made more secure by the addition of a password
USP – unique selling proposition	The features of a product which make it different to the products offered for sale by competitors
Variable cost	The business cost which will change if the level of production changes. Also known as direct cost
Vector-based file	An image file which stores the object as a sequence of commands. Requires less memory than a bitmap file
Virus	Software which is designed to disrupt the normal workings of a computer system
Voice-mail	A method of storing telephone messages on a computer system
Wage	A payment to an employee which is based on a measure of output such as time or the number of items produced
WAN – wide area network	A computer network spread over a large area so that a temporary connection to the network is made when access is required
Website	A collection of web pages that are linked together under one index page
Word-processor	Software which enables the user to create and edit text-based documents
Work-flow analysis	The study of how a business process is carried out. The aim is to change the operation so that it becomes more efficient
World wide web	The name for the linking of web pages on different websites using hyperlinks

Index